Life as a Playwright

A SURVIVAL GUIDE

Jon Klein

methuen | drama

LONDON · NEW YORK · OXFORD · NEW DELHI · SYDNEY

METHUEN DRAMA
Bloomsbury Publishing Plc
50 Bedford Square, London, WC1B 3DP, UK

BLOOMSBURY, METHUEN DRAMA and the Methuen Drama logo are
trademarks of Bloomsbury Publishing Plc

First published in Great Britain 2018

Cover design: Avni Patel

A catalogue record for this book is available from the British Library.

A catalog record for this book is available from the Library of Congress.

ISBN: PB: 978-1-4742-8509-4
ePDF: 978-1-4742-8510-0
eBook: 978-1-4742-8511-7

Typeset by Deanta Global Publishing Services, Chennai, India
Printed and bound in Great Britain

To find out more about our authors and books visit www.bloomsbury.com
and sign up for our newsletters.

To Laura, my wife and fellow playwright,
with love and gratitude

Contents

11 Final Thoughts 169

Introduction

What Is This Book?

Good question. Allow me to explain . . . by telling you what it's *not*.

This is *not* a book about how to write a play. There are too many of those books already, and I've found many of them do more harm than good for beginning playwrights, by emphasizing subjective "rules" that must not be broken, under threat of death. I do have my own thoughts and suggestions about writing plays, but they will arrive in a somewhat scattered fashion while reading this book.

In my opinion, two common-sense books that *do* describe effective methods of playwriting are *The Art and Craft of Playwriting* by Jeffrey Hatcher, and *Backwards and Forwards* by David Ball. Or at the very least, please read *The Poetics* by Aristotle (history's first dramatic theorist). The iconic playwright David Mamet has said that *The Poetics* is the only writing manual any playwright needs. I think he could be right, at least about that.

So if you're sitting in a comfy chair near the Drama section of some brick-and-mortar bookstore (assuming there are such stores hanging on, and also assuming they'd be enlightened enough to stock this particular book), drinking your cappuccino and seeking advice on How to Write a Play, put this book back on the shelf where you found it and buy one from the short list I just mentioned instead. There—I just saved you both time and money. You're welcome, and good luck to you.

Nor is this a book that will tell you the Guaranteed Secret to a Successful Playwriting Career. Any actual working playwright will tell you that there are at least four words wrong with that phrase. More about that later, if you're still with me.

Finally, this is not a book like any other book about playwriting that's out there, as far as I can surmise. Because I don't want it to be. This is not a textbook, a rule book, or a book that discusses play mechanics at length.

So what *is* this book? This is the sort of book I wish had been available to *me* when I was starting out—a book based on experience, not theory. This book will prepare you—to the best of my ability—to *be* a playwright. No one prepared me, or gave me the slightest advice; I had to learn every step on my own, quite often the hard way by making mistakes. And though it was undeniably instructive, I wouldn't say it was the most pleasant way to learn. I hope I can offer an alternative method to you.

I've been teaching and mentoring beginning playwrights for nearly thirty years, and I've noticed that very few of them have the slightest conception about what it's like to be a playwright, or—to slightly revise that phrase—what the life of a playwright might be *like*. And I maintain that's as important, if not more so, than figuring out how to write a wonderful play. Because if you have a wonderful play (and I hope you do, or will produce one soon), that's only the first phase of the battle.

That's often what being a playwright can feel like: a battle. And that's also why, as the title of this book suggests, the most important skill for any playwright is to learn how to *survive*. If I can survive as a playwright, so can you. That brings me to what must be your next natural question . . . who am I to advise you?

I am a playwright.

And I want you to be able to say the same. If you're not ready to proclaim it at this point, then I want to help you get there. Maybe even by the end of this book.

During one forlorn and floundering fall in the late 1970s, as a short-term graduate student studying Dramatic Theory at City University of New York, I was fortunate to be enrolled in a class with the iconic director, critic, and teacher, Harold Clurman. I don't remember a single thing about any other class I took that semester, but I remember his vividly. And Clurman "taught" us nothing. We were tested on various plays and essays, but he didn't bother to spend any class time discussing any of that material.

Instead, he told stories: stories about living in a crummy French apartment with composer Aaron Copland, about seeing the Moscow Art Theatre firsthand, about starting the Group Theater with Cheryl Crawford and Lee Strasberg, about his own wife, Stella Adler, and about working with folks such as Elia Kazan, Clifford Odets, and Uta Hagen. I don't know how many of these names you recognize, but I can tell you these were all seminal figures in the history of the American Theatre. Who cared if Clurman didn't have a lot to say about Shakespeare or Samuel Beckett, even if they were on the syllabus? Instead, he talked about his early days in theatre, and the people he met along the way. I could not have imagined a more inspirational and instructive class, in my own formative years as a theatre artist.

Emulating Clurman, I'm hoping to use my own lessons learned through experience, to inspire beginning playwrights (though hopefully with a bit more organization). Some of those experiences I will share with enthusiasm, but a few of them will be downright embarrassing to reveal. Cautionary tales, so to speak, which can be the most effective lessons of all.

And I'll also mention some of the people I've met at those intersections, some of whose names you may also recognize, who contributed to my own path toward becoming a professional playwright. No writer ever makes the journey alone. I owe the people that I will mention substantial debts of gratitude, and acknowledge their invaluable assistance. (There's also a few I'll mention who were downright adversarial; you'll notice I won't be mentioning them by name, though I certainly could. Those lessons, though negative, were crucial ones as well.)

Finally, at the end of the book, I've invited several prominent American playwrights to submit their own tales of how they established themselves as dramatic writers, and lessons they learned along the way. To my surprise, almost everyone I asked was anxious to contribute to this book, which is why I ended up with a mother lode of seventeen interviews. Their responses are completely verbatim, and reflect a diversity of experiences in the American theatre—because that's where we all started, and where we continue to do most of our work.

Now I should address one likely question, so you'll have some confidence about the authenticity and reliability of what's to come.

Who Am I?

As I mentioned, I'm a playwright. I'm not especially famous. Chances are you've never heard of me, unless you've seen one of my plays in an American regional theater. I've even had two or three critics (along with several students) ask, "How come I've never heard of you?" So you won't hurt my feelings by asking the same question.

Not that any ordinary person would recognize most playwrights' names in this day and age, even if they have had extraordinary success on Broadway. Yasmina Reza, anyone? She is the number one female playwright in the world, with more stage productions to her credit than any other single woman (her plays include *God of Carnage* and *Art*). And there's a handful of recent playwrights who've demonstrated brilliance; happily, many of those are women (Annie Baker, Lauren Gunderson,

Katori Hall, Lynn Nottage, Suzan-Lori Parks, Theresa Rebeck, Sarah Ruhl, etc.). But if I mention any of those names to my non-theatre friends, I'll get blank stares.

And I'm not as well-known as any of them. I'm more of a working stiff playwright—someone who may not be a star, but who has managed to scrape out a living as a playwright for the last thirty years. As of this writing, I've written well over thirty plays, and all but a few of them have been professionally produced—some just once, some many times over, at some of the most renowned regional theaters in the United States. I've won numerous grants and fellowships, which helped to keep me afloat in the lean years. So despite my aversion to blowing my own horn, I think it's safe to say I'm moderately "successful."

I say "moderately" because I've had my share of professional ups and downs (which you'll be reading about shortly). And as I suggested earlier, "success" is a very tricky word, especially in theatre. For now, suffice it to say that what I used to think of as Success—or what you may *currently* think of as Success—ain't necessarily so.

1 Becoming a Playwright

Which Road Should You Take?

There is no clear road. To be honest with you, no road at all.

My two favorite autobiographies of playwrights are Tennessee Williams's *Memoirs,* unsparing in its confessional frankness (not much about playwriting here, but plenty about his sexual adventures and obsessions); and Moss Hart's *Act One*—recently adapted into a Broadway play—which is hilarious and self-deprecating (and may well contain the first mention of a playwright vomiting in the bathroom before the show starts). Both are highly entertaining, but you probably won't learn a lot that you can personally use as you create your own path. Nor will the fascinating biographies of iconic playwrights such as Henrik Ibsen, Anton Chekhov, or even Harold Pinter (all essential reading for other reasons) offer you much guidance on the routes to becoming a produced playwright in the twenty-first century.

In addition, keep in mind that renown as a playwright may occur in sudden, singular achievements without any training or preparation: the Pulitzer Prize–winning plays *Wit* by Margaret Edson and *The Gin Game* by D. L. Coburn are notable examples.

As you can see, it's a hard task to detect any specific formulas for "success." On the other hand, all the playwrights listed above had their own learning experiences—some triumphant, some painful—as well as the thousands of writers I have not yet mentioned—including *you*. But as divergent as all those paths may be, there is still a bit of common ground to be found.

No matter who you are, where you live, or whatever your age, any discussion of playwriting as a profession consists of three perennial struggles: (1) trying to get noticed, (2) trying to get produced, and (3) trying to avoid unexpected disasters once you've achieved (1) and (2). All playwrights have their own individual journeys, but they intersect at those three junctions.

Over the years I've learned that "success" is subject to Einsteinian principles of relativity. For example, long-term success often includes the vital experience of failure. Among my productions, I've had hits, and I've had flops. And in some ways, the flops were more instructive—more crucial to my development as an artist. Sounds strange? It is. I'll explain what I mean in subsequent chapters, but I hope you can accept this principle:

Success equals Survival.   **!**

A life as a playwright is a roller coaster ride. And it's not for everyone—many folks just aren't equipped to ride roller coasters. There can be thrills, exhilaration, and joy in the sudden, unpredictable climbs. But there may also be equally sudden dives to the ground, wrenching turns, and long, painful struggles to climb back up. To rephrase the well-known adage referring to old age, playwriting ain't for sissies. The utter impossibility for any playwright to effectively predict their future path is perhaps the most daunting aspect—daunting for anyone in the arts, of course, but the nature of working in theatre often results in, well, more *drama*.

My own family and friends often wondered about my "weird" choice of profession. It is still an odd choice to most people, I'm sure. Dramatic writing can be highly profitable—but usually not in the theatre. Screenwriters and television writers can be paid highly; they have unions that guarantee minimum fees that are fairly generous. But playwrights don't have a union; those who make anything close to a living wage in the theatre alone are rare birds indeed.

Another old cliché, attributed to playwright Robert Anderson, is that you can make a killing in the theatre, but you can't make a living. I sometimes ask young people what they think a playwright's income might be. I can get answers that suggest a hundred thousand dollars or more. Per *year*. After I stop laughing (and see that they're not), my reply is usually, "Um . . . no."

Perhaps Hollywood is at fault, perpetuating those old 1930s celluloid fantasies that displayed imaginary playwrights living in palatial penthouse apartments in Manhattan, with the ability to travel on ocean cruises around the world, staying in luxury hotels in Paris or Rome. I remember howling with laughter (along with all my writer friends) during the 2003 movie *Something's Gotta Give*, when we were introduced to the gigantic Hamptons "beach house" that playwright Diane Keaton owned. Not likely.

Even the most successful playwrights, from Tony Kushner to the late August Wilson, have spoken about the impossibility of subsisting solely on playwriting income. If you have any doubts about that notion, feel free to read Todd London's depressingly enlightening 2009 book, *Outrageous Fortune*. I quote his research here regarding playwriting income: "An average playwright, making $39,000 a year (the top end of average), might make $14,700 (49 percent) from playwriting-related work, $5,850 (15 percent) from their plays generally, and $1,170 from production royalties. At the bottom end of average, the reward would be $12,250 from work related to playwriting, $3,750 from the plays themselves, and a paltry $750 from royalties."[1] Like the rest of American income, I don't believe those numbers have risen significantly in the last half-decade.

Bummer, eh? Some critics, most notably Chris Jones of the *Chicago Tribune*, characterized the playwrights interviewed

---

[1]Todd London, Ben Pesner, and Zannie Giraud Voss. *Outrageous Fortune: The Life and times of the New American Play*. New York, NY: Theatre Development Fund, 2009. Print.

in that book as "whiners."[2] Still, I strongly suggest you read *Outrageous Fortune* as an essential companion to this one, so you'll get a fuller understanding of what choosing to be a playwright really means.

The decision to become a playwright can be the start of a wonderful journey. It can also mean a very rough trip, full of road closures and detours. And to go back to that phrase I debunked ("Guaranteed Secret to a Successful Playwriting Career")—it's time for you to learn that when it comes to playwriting, there are no Guarantees, there are very few Secrets, there's infrequent and fleeting evidence of Success, and there's little resemblance to what most people could possibly call a Career.

So what's the attraction? What could possibly compel anyone to pursue such an uncertain existence, short of masochism? Some very strong reasons, I think, which I'll discuss. But before I do, it's a good idea for you to take stock of your own goals at this point. So I hope you'll allow me to ask you the following question:

Why Do You Want to Be a Playwright?

Not knowing you personally, I can't and won't speculate about your personal reasons. I'm just telling you that it's a very important question for you to ask yourself. By the time you finish this book, you may throw it across the room and feel like I talked you out of pursuing a life as a playwright. If so, I'm sorry. But let's face it. If I (or anyone else) can talk you out of it, then it's probably for the best. You're not as dedicated to the idea as you thought you were. If, however, you're more determined than ever to beat the odds, then you, my friend, have what it takes to continue, full speed ahead. And you'll have a better shot at doing well.

---

[2]Patrick Healey. "Playwrights' Nurturing Is the Focus of a Study." *New York Times:* January 13, 2010: n. pag. Print.

Determination is the most important attribute of any playwright. !

So what reasons are there to pursue such an uncertain and speculative vocation? I've already said it can't be about the money, because there usually isn't much of that. Why do it at all, then?

The simple answer, of course, is that people who consciously choose difficult professions—once they get a taste of them—cannot envision themselves doing anything else. Why else do actors persist in what is probably the most frustrating occupation on earth? (Many of them turn to playwriting, so that gives you an idea of *their* levels of frustration.)

In addition, there are two consistent aspects to playwriting that have undeniable appeal to those who dabble in dramatic writing:

a **The Spoken Word.** The ancient art of storytelling has never lost its power and appeal. And some people have had special facility for it, whether they were prophets speaking in parables, balladeers telling tales of honor and chivalry, or Greek and Elizabethan playwrights dramatizing the fall of kings. If you have a keen interest in the way people struggle to communicate, and have a certain facility for imitating their language and conversation, then you know how enjoyable it is to hear your own words delivered to an audience. And that brings me to the second—even more important—reason.

b **The Audience.** Nothing matches the excitement of a live audience, especially for those who create work for their benefit. Whether you're a theatre performer, director, designer, or writer, none of your work will have full impact and significance until an audience witnesses it. A child will sing and dance for an audience of one—maybe a pet if no one else is available—because there's an inherent human desire to be seen and heard, beginning with our first stumbling steps across the floor. And a live performance, whether it's for a few people sitting around a table or a couple thousand people in a Broadway theater, has an addictive quality for dramatists. Novelists, poets, and journalists can only *assume* someone is reading their work. Playwrights see and hear the impact of their writing firsthand, and can experience the thrill of affecting an audience (as well as the humiliation of boring them, which occasionally goes with the territory).

Here's another list for you. I've noticed some common characteristics that apply to people who love theatre, and are drawn to work for, on or behind the stage. Maybe you will find yourself in one of the three following categories:

a Those who are introduced to theatre at a younger age, by family members or mentors who themselves worked in the field. This early input can provide comfort and excitement in a world that many folks can find a bit alien.

b Those who are urged by the burning desires to address social issues and political urges through the immediacy of live theatre. Both personal experience and studied observations impel these artists to write, direct and/or perform.

c Those who need an outlet for confronting their emotional needs, such as self-esteem, loneliness, depression, or any other personal issues that may result in marginalization. Oddballs and misfits have historically been attracted to the theatre.

Or, of course, some combination of two or three. Me? I'm primarily in the last group, and fine with it. No violins required.

I had no theatre background in my family: my father owned a machine shop, and my mother was a nurse, then a homemaker once she married. My siblings were drawn to engineering and law. There was no theatergoing in my family—none, never. So obviously no guidance, just a lot of strange looks and comments like, "I hope you know what you're doing." (By the way—I didn't.)

Nor did I have much social or political awareness, at least not as a child. What I did have was a voracious appetite for books, and I was reading them from the age of three. I had severe asthmatic allergies that prevented me from doing much outside of the house. So I spent most of my time in my bedroom, reading anything I could get my hands on. Most writers begin as heavy readers, I believe. I probably spent more time in the world of my own imagination than I did in the real one.

Eventually I started to enjoy reading those books out loud, especially the ones that contained dialogue. And like most children (I'm thinking of Andy in the wonderful movie *Toy Story*), I started enacting little plays with my toys. Children are the most open, devoted theatre audiences for just this reason: they're watching other people "play," just as they do in their own bedrooms and backyards.

Finally—in the fifth grade, if I remember correctly—I was assigned my first play to read in school. It was a bizarre choice, but one that had great impact on me: Marc Connelly's Pulitzer Prize–winning play from 1930, *Green Pastures*. Although it ran five years on Broadway, and became a film in 1936, today it suffers in reputation due to its racial stereotypes. *Green Pastures* depicts Heaven as one eternal fish fry in the Deep South, populated by angels (and God Himself) who are all portrayed as African American. A strange assignment indeed, considering I was attending a white Catholic school in a German American neighborhood. But I would like to give the nun who assigned it the benefit of the doubt, since the content is very respectful of the spiritual values of its designated people, even if it painted those characters too broadly.

Whatever the reason it was assigned, I was fascinated by the dialogue, in which Connelly tried to spell out regional dialects. It made no sense to me on the page—I had to read it out loud to understand how the words sounded. I read it over and over, aloud to myself. Thus, as a child, did I begin to learn the power and music of the spoken word. To this day, I always read plays out loud whenever possible—especially my own.

Influenced by Connelly's play, I was inspired to try writing one myself. Having been given the homework assignment to "write a story," I decided to create an event using nothing but dialogue (or "talking," which is what I called it). It was basically a sketch about an auction that gets out of control—why an auction, I don't know. But since we were supposed to read our stories out loud, I performed a dozen or so characters by myself. The success of this skit with the class must have shocked my teacher, because before I knew it I was "on tour," performing the piece for each and every class in the school, from first to eighth. Before that moment, I was dismissed as the weird brainiac who somehow skipped the fourth grade. Suddenly I was an entertainer in demand, at the age of nine. This event changed my status at school, both with my classmates and with the teachers. I was beginning to learn something, very early on, about the give-and-take relationship between performers and audience—why that is a special relationship, and how it can have impact.

That's a lesson I learned as a kid. Now keep in mind I was an extremely shy child, a scrawny asthmatic kid with glasses, who endured verbal and physical bullying on a regular basis. Yet somehow I found the ability to acquire self-confidence and positive attention—as long as I could be *someone else*. It didn't matter whether I was reading a role from a book or play, or performing a character in my own bedroom or (later on) in front of hundreds of paying strangers. It felt good to be able to step into someone else's shoes, if only for a little while. Later on, when I started writing multiple characters and using them to tell prolonged stories in a theatre, the principle remained the same; the only difference was that I could try on many kinds of shoes at once.

That "good feeling" is a real one. It's the reason that theatre can be therapeutic for so many people, and why people continue to be drawn to its allure. Of course, it's important to get past those therapeutic origins, in order to hone and craft one's skills and become a better artist. But the beginnings are often marked by the unexpected discovery of how it feels to receive approval and admiration from those who would not ordinarily express it. I think it's important to remember those first steps and realize their proper significance in the development of a theatre artist.

Most adult playwrights can point to similar experiences in their youth, when artistic achievements of some small note gave them a little extra juice. But it doesn't have to be directly connected to writing plays, not right away. I didn't write another play until I was twenty-five years old. Instead, I pursued my urge to perform, not only as an actor but also as a musician.

I began to study classical guitar, then like most kids back then, turned to rock. That led to a garage band that played pop music for weddings, bar mitzvahs, and bowling banquets (yes, like Adam Sandler in the movie *The Wedding Singer*). It was good money, and I continued to learn about performing: the structure of an hour-long set, the rhythms of song selection and order, the energy of an audience, and their ebbs and flows of boredom and attention. All these are contributing factors to understanding live performance, even as a teenager.

Do you remember the first play you ever saw?   ❗

Chances are, if you're younger than me (and I hope you are), your first exposure to theatre was a play written and performed primarily for young audiences. There has been a remarkable multiplicity of children's theatre in the last thirty years, and many schools now take kids to see plays on a regular basis. But that was not the case when I was young. The wonderful organization Stage One had not yet been formed in my hometown of Louisville, Kentucky. Fortunately, there was a professional theater in town, and it was a significant one that was beginning to achieve national prominence: Actors Theatre of Louisville (ATL), which was at that time under the leadership of its newly appointed Artistic Director, Jon Jory.

That theater (and that man) would have a profound effect on my professional development later in life, but for a long while it was a place I had heard of but never attended. Until a friend of mine talked me into going with him on a student discount; that's when I saw my very first play, when I was a junior in high school. And no, it wasn't *Our Town*, or *Romeo and Juliet*, or *A Christmas Carol*, or any of the typical choices for primary theatre experiences. Believe it or not, the very first play I ever saw was *Marat/Sade* by Peter Weiss. More formally known by its full title, *The Persecution and Assassination of Jean-Paul Marat as Performed by the Inmates of the Asylum of Charenton Under the Direction of the Marquis de Sade,* this play within a play shows the infamous Marquis de Sade directing a play about a famous political murder—set in an insane asylum. Fun for all ages! What was my reaction, at such a young and sheltered age of fifteen? I was completely blown away.

At this time, ATL had not moved to its present location in the vault of an old bank building. Back then, ATL was occupying an old, abandoned train station (from the days when passenger trains actually came through Louisville). It was a dark, dreary, and scary place—more suited for a haunted house than a theater, really—and therefore perfect for the setting of Jon Jory's brilliant production. He used the technique of "breaking the fourth wall" in an ingenious way, by having inmates of the asylum scattered throughout the audience. Since I was seated in the front row of the balcony, I was fortunate enough (if you can call it that) to have one of those drooling, cackling inmates right next to me, locked in a small cage. And he spent much of the performance staring at me, grunting, and once even fingering my shirt from between his bars. I was terrified, of course, as well as utterly thrilled. To this day I cannot forget the amazing visceral effect of that production, which introduced me to the power of live theatre for the very first time.

As a result of that astounding show, I was hooked on theatre for life. But I didn't really know how to participate. Writing a script still hadn't occurred to me; that was something *writers* did, and I by no means could conceive of myself being anything like that. So instead, I began my theatrical career the way most young people do—as an actor, which I attempted to become all the way through high school and college. You have probably done some of the same. And if you haven't, you've missed out on some very important training toward being a dramatist.

I can't say how good I was (who can, when you're usually playing roles that are twenty to forty years older than you are), but these experiences helped me to overcome my crippling shyness, and gave me public confidence and assurance. And I got a taste of what it's like to perform, which is something every writer needs to try at least once or twice. After all, you're writing for actors!

So far, still no inclination to be a playwright. I still knew very little about theatre, other than that I enjoyed acting. In my freshman year of college, at the age of seventeen (I mentioned skipping the fourth grade, right?), I landed the plum role of Buffalo Bill in Arthur Kopit's brilliant Vietnam allegory, *Indians*. This understandably caused a lot of resentment among the older actors in the Drama Department, some of whom had been studying for three or four years and had fully expected to be awarded the part. There was a lot of hostility toward me during rehearsals, and I found myself ostracized. This was the beginning of my disillusionment with being an actor. The other factors were my increasing sense that I couldn't maintain interest and freshness in a part that I was forced to repeat on a nightly basis—without fully understanding that my boredom indicated my own superficiality and limited ability. All except for the famous ending of the play, when Buffalo Bill is reduced to selling Native American trinkets to the audience. I stepped off the stage and approached the people on the aisle seats. Some were simply embarrassed, but some were in tears and some seemed quite angry.

I realized something important then. I was by no means a very good actor at the age of seventeen—honestly, I had a decent voice but not much physical control. I was way too young for the role and not especially brilliant at it. But the audience was emotionally affected. And I realized it had little to do with me—I was learning the effect of a wonderful, powerful play. It was the writing! I also realized, as I wandered through the audience and experienced their diverse emotions firsthand, that it was the place to be. The *audience* is where I felt electricity and meaning—not up on the stage. After *Indians*, I continued to act in various roles, but found myself decreasingly enthusiastic about being onstage.

Despite my participation in a contemporary play, playwriting was still something that I associated with ancient dead people, like Molière or Ibsen. Until an eye-opening excursion to Manhattan—a class trip to see New York theatre between my junior and senior years of college. In case this seems extravagant, keep in mind that at that time, I was able to see these shows for about $25 each! I saw two extraordinary musicals: Bob Fosse's production of *Pippin*, and Harold Prince's circus-inspired production of *Candide*. These were outstanding examples of sheer theatricality at their best. And on that same trip, I saw several amazing plays on Broadway: Eugene O'Neill's *A Moon for the Misbegotten* with Jason Robards and Colleen Dewhurst; David Rabe's *The Boom Boom Room*, with Jill Clayburgh; Peter Shaffer's renowned play *Equus*, starring Anthony Hopkins and Tom Hulce; and John Wood in Tom Stoppard's dazzling play *Travesties*.

Seeing such legendary shows at such a young age sealed my fate. After such a trip, how could I have felt anything but inspiration and determination to enter this crazy but exhilarating life of the theatre?

Even so, none of those were the show that had the greatest effect on me. I went Off-Broadway to see a play by a young playwright who had suddenly garnered a lot of attention for his fresh, irreverent look at college-age students, approximately my own age, living in a communal house. I had just finished a similar experience, living in my own communal house with disparate types of students (male and female), in my junior year of college. It was Michael Weller's *Moonchildren* that made me realize once and for all that there were living writers who were writing about things close to my own experience—and that just maybe I could do it too!

But I still hadn't reached the point of being able to call myself a playwright, even in my wildest dreams.

As I said earlier, I came to playwriting relatively late compared to some others, and wouldn't even think about writing a play until I was twenty-four years old. That's not particularly unusual, though. August Wilson (whom I first knew when he was primarily a poet) didn't receive his first professional production until the age of thirty-six. That's the same age that George Bernard Shaw wrote his first play. And don't forget good old Samuel Beckett, who wrote his first play (which remains unproduced) at the age of forty-one, a year before he began to write *Waiting for Godot*.

The magic threshold is different for everyone. When will you cross over? Meaning . . .

When Do You Call Yourself a Playwright?

Some folks say it takes years of writing scripts. Others insist it doesn't happen until you have your first professional production. For me, the answer is simpler and sooner: it happens *when you write a play*.

The Dramatists Guild of America (DGA), the service organization for American playwrights, recently revised their membership eligibility to include non-produced playwrights. It used to be a more exclusive club, only available to those writers who managed to secure productions in New York or prominent regional theaters. But realizing the current difficulty in achieving such status, the Guild relaxed their admission requirements. To quote from their website:

> *To qualify for the new Member level, a writer must have had work either professionally produced or published by an established publisher. Professional production is no longer defined by the size of the theater but simply by whether tickets were sold to the public. All playwrights, composers, lyricists and librettists interested in Guild membership, but who do not meet one of the above criteria, may join at the Associate level.*[3]

That means their definition of a playwright—or at least an "Associate" playwright—is even more lenient than my own. According to the DGA, you're a playwright if you *say* you are—and pay the membership fee, of course.

Critics take a sterner attitude. They spend every day trying to weed out the "wannabe" playwrights from the real ones, who are ordained as having "arrived." But their designations can be unpredictable. Although they are always looking for the next

---

[3]"Dramatists Guild | Info." *Dramatists Guild | Info.* N.p., n.d. Web. November 10, 2014.

theatrical phenomenon, occasionally they may champion an unknown author who has a play performed in an under-the-radar fringe theater. Unfortunately, the odds of getting *any* review in a small theater are nearly insurmountable, at a time when print media is purging staff in draconian budget cuts.

Think critics are tough? Try getting the Internal Revenue Service to agree that your profession is playwriting! They generally insist that in order for you to claim deductible expenses as a playwright, you have to show a *profit*. Otherwise you can't declare it a profession at all—it's a *hobby*.

The simple truth of it is the following: at some point, in order for you to progress, you'll have to be able to look in the mirror and tell yourself that like it or not, I am a Playwright.

Just don't expect your family or friends to clap their hands in delight. Early responses to my own declaration were along the lines of "Don't be absurd." I've heard gay friends tell me that it was actually easier for them to *come out* to their families than to tell them they wanted to be playwrights. The bottom line: only *you* can decide when, how, or if to make the leap to being a playwright. That moment varies for different people.

I'm sure you know someone who had a calling from an early age for whatever they wanted to do, and set out to do it without doubts or hesitations. It may take some restraint, but try not to hate them. Their decisions may seem easier, but don't be fooled. Those kinds of personalities make folks susceptible to much larger—and much more painful—defeats, when something just happens to go wrong. And if you're human, chances are that will happen more than once.

When it comes to writers, everyone takes a different path. Some have early success and manage to sustain it. Others have early success, and then have trouble repeating it. Others take many years—maybe close to a lifetime—to achieve anything resembling "success." And then there are writers like myself, who have had frequent productions and occasional "breakthroughs" to national attention, but who otherwise have not had a "hit" play (for some reason, "hit plays" aren't usually considered to occur outside of Manhattan). There are more of us than you may think.

The path to life as a playwright can begin at any time, in any place, often unexpectedly. !

Mine began when I made the profoundly wise decision to get real experience at a professional theater. Drama schools (such as the school where I now teach) currently do a much better job of preparing students with practical experience, but my own schooling back in the early 1970s left me unprepared. So I threw caution to the wind and signed up for an internship back at my home town theater, ATL. That meant moving back home, at the age of 24, and living with my parents—something that seemed like a huge sacrifice on my part (and a big imposition to them).

But in the long run, it was the best decision I could have made. And that's where I made my debut as a playwright. I'm going to spend some time on my own introduction to the world of playwriting, in the hopes that you will find a similar way to break through, in your own way. I'll devote much of the next chapter to these events, as well as sharing some thoughts about writing your first play.

At the end of each chapter, beginning here, I would like to repeat and emphasize some helpful comments and suggestions that I mentioned within (just in case I managed to bury the most salient points in my ramblings).

Points to Remember

- Experience is the best teacher in the theatre. Learn from your own, and learn from others.

- Reevaluate your own definition of "Success."

- If you can *survive* as a playwright, that makes you a Successful Playwright.

- As you can read in the recommended book *Outrageous Fortune*, you should have realistic expectations about the income of a typical playwright.

- Given the uncertainty and instability of a playwright's life, it's crucial that you ask yourself *why* you want to be one.

- The two most prominent reasons to pursue a life as a playwright: (1) The Spoken Word, and (2) The Audience.

- Always read your writing out loud. Notice how that changes the dynamics of the writing.

- Don't ever underestimate your relationship with the audience. Don't ignore them, don't "alienate" them—but by all means challenge and entertain them.

- Get comfortable with live audiences of all sizes. Develop your performance and public speaking skills so that you can learn their group dynamics and how to affect them.

- Don't be ashamed of the positive feelings you develop through artistic achievement. Just don't allow that to become the ultimate goal.

- Other kinds of "performing" can be relevant and instructive to beginning playwrights.

- Always remember the play that introduced you to the power of live theatre. What was the effect on you, and how was it achieved? How can you use or duplicate those achievements in your own writing?

- Whenever it's offered, look for opportunities to perform for an audience at any level—amateur or professional. If you can learn to play to an audience, you can learn how to write for them.

- Whenever possible, try to meet living playwrights who are getting their work produced. Don't be shy about asking them tips about how to get your own plays noticed! There will be additional tips on that subject by various playwrights at the end of this book.

- When do you become a playwright? When you *write a play*. Other opinions don't matter.

2 Writing Your First Play

Are You *Compelled* to Write a Play?

You're sitting at your laptop. Or your notebook or your legal pad. And you're staring, and you're thinking, and you're sort of watching CNN in the background, and you're wondering if you should have a morning run, or a late night snack. What you're *not* doing is writing. And you know what? That's okay.

I'm a firm believer that it's probably best to refrain from writing until you have something you want to write about. I know that daily regiments work for some playwrights, getting up two hours early to write before they head to work, or using each and every afternoon before the kids come home from school. And I applaud such regularity and determination. But unless you have something that is absolutely burning in your brain, something that is pleading with you to be written down—in other words, a *passion*—such time and dedication may not be particularly fruitful. Don't beat yourself up for not writing. Let the story itself, or the characters, convince you that there's nothing more important than getting it all down on paper (or computer screen). And listen to *that*.

Many prominent playwrights will talk about their process as one of following orders. Certain characters are nagging them, begging to be brought to life. And those writers know when to listen and obey. I totally concur. I would even go on to suggest that those characters are really the ones *writing* the script itself. They are the ones feeding the author what lines to say and when, and (even more importantly) the ones who object when their lines are inappropriate or contrived.

Listen to your characters, and follow their guidance. That's the best piece of advice I can give you about how to write a memorable play. !

If, on the other hand, you're *not* being compelled to write, it probably means that you don't yet have an effectively dramatic idea, with strong characters. And you probably can't *make* that happen—you may have to wait until it simply *does* happen. That's your cue to sit down and start writing.

As a teacher of dramatic writing, it's ironic for me to talk about the importance of giving yourself enough time to be inspired. The school system is based on unrelenting deadlines; students are expected to be finished with their assignments by the end of the quarter or semester. Such an artificial schedule doesn't always align with the creative process. That's why, time and time again, I have had students who ask if they can abandon their current plays and start over with something they're more excited about.

Nothing pleases me more. Of course I'm not going to tell them, "Sorry. You've only got six weeks left in the semester, so you'd better stick with what you've got." That would be antithetical to everything I feel about playwriting. Their regular weekly writings have led them to something else—something they are more *compelled* to write. That's exactly as it should be. If they're excited, so am I. And they don't care if there's only six weeks left—they write like demons to get it done in time! And they always do. Those new plays are almost always more powerful, more theatrical, and more essential than the ones they began with.

Good writing can come as the result of *not* writing, or even writing the wrong thing. !

These are not things to be avoided. These are aspects of writing itself—periods of creative rejuvenation. I highly recommend a helpful treatise on this subject: *On Writer's Block* by Victoria Nelson. For two decades, this book has kept frustrated or inactive writers from feeling frustrated or guilty. She successfully shows, through anecdotes and examples, that there may be good reasons *not* to write. All creative artists sometimes need time to recharge; it's nothing to worry about.

Are You Ready to Start?

So far, I've been asking you to consider whether you have a need to write, and whether it's important for you to write *right now*. Let's now assume that your answers are strongly affirmative. You have an idea for a new play that is just screaming to be written. An earth-shattering, life-changing idea that you're convinced will be one of the most brilliant plays ever written. Hey—good for you! A great idea is the most important part of writing a new play.

Sorry. I just lied. Oh, how I wish that were true. But great ideas are a dime a dozen, while knowing how to turn them into functioning, effective plays (or novels, or poems, or screenplays) is one of the most difficult things any writer can hope to accomplish. It comprises the difference between an *idea* and a *story*.

F. Scott Fitzgerald famously said, "There are no second acts in American lives."[1] Not many people are aware that he wrote several plays in his early years, but he did. So I've always felt that as an unsuccessful playwright, this is what Fitzgerald was really expressing in that quote: the difference between writing and real life. He knew that in his own life, he had a fantastic "breakthrough" with a highly successful first novel—*This Side of*

---

[1] *The Last Tycoon*, "Hollywood, ETC.," ed. Edmund Wilson (1941).

Paradise—that rapidly pushed him into public consciousness. This was followed by twenty years of unsuccessfully attempting to repeat that success (*The Great Gatsby* didn't become a sensation until after his death). Scott knew from his own life that second acts were hard to accomplish.

And as a playwright, he knew they were hard but *necessary*. Structurally, most plays have three acts—and that second act is a killer. I'm not talking about intermissions—it doesn't matter whether a play has none, one or two—they all usually have a beginning, a middle and an end (according to Aristotle, anyway), thus a three-act structure. And let's face it—*no one* enjoys writing the second act. It's a brutal process to come up with enough obstacles and complications to prolong that difficult middle without making it *seem* prolonged.

Idea versus Story

I'll use an example. Let's say I get an idea for a play. I'll sum it up in one sentence (a logline, to use film parlance).

A brilliant young woman becomes a new US Senator, quickly joining the Foreign Relations Committee, only to discover that her father is spying for the Russians.

Not bad (maybe a bit trite, but let's go with it for now). I know that conflict is crucial to any drama, so it's built into the premise. Now let's say I'm given the chance to pitch my idea to an artistic director and a literary manager at a theater (an unlikely opportunity unless I'm being commissioned, by the way). With enthusiasm and confidence, I give them the description above. Here's their guaranteed response: "And?"

Breaking into a sweat, I think they must want to know the outcome. Thus I offer several possible endings, each equally terrific (or so I think):

a *She talks her father into surrendering to the US authorities.*

b *She resigns her position and escapes with her father to Russia.*

c *A Russian agent has her assassinated.*

d *She makes another discovery—he's not really her father at all.*

I could keep going, but I'll stop there. I check in with my listeners, and instead of being enraptured with my idea, they express dismay. So much for my great idea.

What went wrong? My listeners didn't care about the ending. They wanted to know if I had a *story*. Questions I should have been prepared to answer: Who is this woman? How does she deal with this devastating conflict when she learns the truth? How does she arrive at her final decision? In other words, I spoke of a beginning and an ending, but no middle. What happens in between? And if I don't even care how it ends, why should anyone else?

Here's an idea of something that could comprise the second act:

She tries to keep the Feds from making the same discovery, all the while trying to protect her own new career.

That suggests complications and obstacles—two aspects of drama that are essential, especially to a second act. I still don't have a play, of course. But I may have the bare bones of a play. Now I will need to flesh it out in such a way that leads inevitably to the final conclusion, which is one that my lead character cares about enormously and will affect all her decisions.

I realize what I have to do. My own method will involve a plot outline (in my head if not on paper), a full understanding of the characters and their relationships, and how their desires and conflicts drive their decisions. And I'll require a lot of help from my characters along the way, listening to them about what seems appropriate to their characters or way off base.

Finally, I need to pay attention to what changes during the course of the play. Do the characters end up in a different place—emotionally or circumstantially—than they began? In dramatic terminology, do they *arc*?

As you can tell, much easier said than done.

These are essential aspects of the first draft of any piece of dramatic writing. The details of plot and character can be added in subsequent drafts. But for your writing to be recognized as a first draft,

You must have a beginning, a middle, and an end, as well as characters that change. You're not telling a story otherwise. ❗

I also stay aware of impulses to *change* my story while writing it. It may be because I become more interested in an alternative plot, or perhaps minor characters begin to interest me more. Not only is that okay, but it's also probably a good sign. I'll follow those impulses if they intrigue me.

I should mention that there are prominent playwrights who may bristle with my emphasis on plot and character elements. What about, they may ask, *Waiting for Godot*? There's a play that doesn't seem to have much of a plot, if any. And the characters don't seem to change at all. Would I dare suggest *that* isn't a play? I would never declare such a thing about one of the most powerful and influential plays ever written. But I disagree with the premise that Beckett's play is exempt from plot and character arcs. The plot is a deceptively simple one, but it's one that uses suspense, surprise, anticipation, and a connected sequence of events—what Aristotle himself described as plot. And I submit that the characters do go through emotional change, even if their circumstances seem to come full circle. Didi and Gogo are not the same people at the end that they were at the beginning. Profound changes—from *within*—take place during the course of that play.

I will grant you that what I've briefly described above as the essential elements of a play may seem mechanical or formulaic. But I also believe that stories can be told any number of ways and in any variety of styles. Still, despite the endless debates about the nature of storytelling, I do think people come to the theatre to have wonderful tales told to them and to be emotionally affected as a result. The various dramatic methods are up to you.

So how do you learn more about those methods? Beginning writers don't suffer from a lack of passion as much as a lack of know-how. How do you go about writing a play, if you've never tried?

How Do You Learn About Playwriting Methods?

As I mentioned, I'm not going to get too much into the nitty-gritty of play structure, character arcs, and skillful dialogue. That's not the focus of this book. But I do have several thoughts about how to acquire training in the craft of playwriting.

There are six possible routes to consider, at least in the United States. You can decide which is most appealing and practical for you.

A **College and Graduate Programs.** If searching for a college or graduate program, be sure to pick one that gives you valuable experience on the rehearsal floor, and performance opportunities—not just the words on a page. My own MFA Playwriting program at Catholic University in DC (for example) offers the chance for full thesis productions, included in the regular mainstage season and directed by local professionals from the DC theatre community. But be careful about taking on student debt. You will not find quick opportunities to pay back your school loans as you struggle to establish yourself as a playwright in your postgraduate years. (That's why I only take two students a year in my own program, so that they may both receive full tuition fellowships. Two a year is all we can provide.)

B **Low-Residency Programs**. There are also low-residency programs that allow you to pursue an MFA degree in Playwriting, by attending classes six weeks a summer for three to five years. Two examples (where I myself have taught) are the programs run by Hollins University in Roanoke, Virginia, and Spalding University in Louisville, Kentucky. There are others of course; do your research.

C **Online and Extension Programs**. Due to the expense of college programs, there are cheaper alternatives when studying the art and craft of playwriting. More and more major universities offer online classes, usually taught by strong professional playwrights who are supplementing their writing income in a way that doesn't interfere too highly with their own work. In addition, there are a wealth of extension or certificate programs that teach dramatic writing for stage, screen, and TV. Having taught at two of them, at the University of Washington and UCLA, I can assure you that these are terrific ways to immerse yourself and learn the basics of dramatic writing in six to ten weeks. To mention another new example, in response to the need for affordable training in playwriting, the DGA is embarking on a new venture called The Dramatists Guild Institute of Dramatic Writing, in which they are offering various classes in person in their New York offices, as well as online.[2]

---

[2]http://www.dginstitute.org

D Internships at Professional Theaters that specialize in New Play Programs. The advantage is that you can see professional playwrights hone their craft in person, on stage. I credit my own experiences at ATL with more value than my college experience. Financially, you generally do not pay for internships, but you will still need to find ways of financing your housing and personal expenses. (I was lucky enough to return to home during my internship at ATL, and lucky enough to have parents who tolerated my postgraduate return.)

E Playwrights' Groups and Associations. If you can make it through their application processes, the two most important membership organizations are New Dramatists in New York, and the Playwrights' Center in Minneapolis (which was my most important learning experience after ATL). You will have the opportunity to meet and commune with other playwrights who are developing their own work, and learn by observation and participation. In addition, many of them provide classes, either in person or online. There are, of course, several other playwriting groups in other cities and states.

F Teach Yourself. Although I put this one last, it's the most important of all. See and read as many plays as you possibly can! Constant exposure to a wide diversity of plays and theatre styles is the best foundation for any dramatic writer (and don't ignore the overlapping formats of film and television).

So as a playwriting professor, how important do I believe formal, academic training to be? I'll tell you a secret. I never took a playwriting class in my life. Neither did Edward Albee, nor August Wilson. None of the most famous playwrights of yesteryear—Arthur Miller, Tennessee Williams, Lillian Hellman, Harold Pinter—took playwriting classes, because there were none to take! Nor did some of the writers who write about their early experiences at the end of this book. Like them, I learned the craft entirely through other methods. As for me, the most valuable experience I acquired was through my internship at ATL.

My Internship

ATL is now considered one of the country's paramount regional theaters, but at the time I interned there (in the late 1970s), it was only starting to get national attention. That was due to the visionary efforts of its relatively new Artistic Director, Jon Jory. Jory had already brought challenging work to Kentucky (such as the aforementioned *Marat/Sade*), but for the last couple of years he had been slowly introducing a new concept: to use his theater as a place to premiere new work. As a result of his efforts, most of the new play programs that are currently operating across the country owe their ideas to the place where it all began: Actors Theatre of Louisville.

What is now internationally known as the Humana Festival began without corporate sponsorship and on a much smaller scale. ATL's new play festival began in 1977, as two plays were produced that had won a competition called the Great American Play Contest. Although this was a modest beginning, one of the two plays was a sudden hit that became widely known: D. L. Coburn's *The Gin Game*. Word of mouth brought the estimable married actors Hume Cronyn and Jessica Tandy to Louisville, where they quickly secured the rights to a Broadway production. Before long, Coburn won the Pulitzer Prize, and ATL suddenly received national attention as a place to discover new plays.

Just to show that success was no fluke, Louisville native Marsha Norman had a startlingly powerful entry the following year: *Getting Out*. That show also went on to acclaim in New

York, and Jory's little play festival suddenly became a very big deal indeed. I joined up as an apprentice the following year, in 1979, not realizing that I was to become part of a large expansion of an important new play festival, now under the sponsorship of Louisville-based health-care company Humana. There was a lot more money behind the festival now, with a lot more national attention, and the stakes were high. Unbelievably, that year introduced yet another Pulitzer Prize-winning author—the third in a row (though to be precise, Norman was to win hers a little later with *Night, Mother*). Beth Henley's *Crimes of the Heart* was instantly successful, was fast-tracked to Broadway, quickly won the Pulitzer, and became a feature film. I was there in the midst of the biggest, best Humana Festival to date—perhaps the most influential experience of my life.

Why do I say that? Well, first of all, Jory assigned to us the Herculean task of finding every person in the United States— if not the entire world—who was writing plays. And beyond that, to determine which ones were *any good*. That's no exaggeration—as a literary intern, it was entrusted to me (and my co-intern, Lee Johnson, under the tutelage of literary manager Elizabeth King) to solicit, receive, and read literally hundreds of scripts in the year I was there.

What Does the Reader Look For?

Reading that many plays, I quickly began to understand the elements that made some plays immediately stand out from the others. And I learned the importance of grabbing the reader within the first ten pages of the script!

As any hopeful dramatist should realize, you have to attract the reader's attention very quickly in dramatic writing, so that the script will be moved from the towering "reject" pile to the much smaller "further consideration" pile. How to accomplish this? By distinguishing yourself in one or more of the following methods:

a Powerful conflict, introduced early on in the script.

b A new or unusual "voice," indicating an original approach to dramatic dialogue or structure.

c The creation of developed, fascinating characters that actors will desperately want to portray, introduced quickly.

One play I found in my reading caught my attention, and I forwarded it on to special consideration by Jory. It was a play that met all the criteria above, and met them quickly as I read it. That play was *Extremities* by William Mastrosimone—and in what was becoming a regular pattern, it was included in the following year's festival, where it was picked up for a New York production and eventual film version. That play was about a would-be rapist who has the tables turned on him, and difficult questions about justice and retribution are raised. Tough stuff— but the subject matter alone wouldn't have made it stand out from the hundreds of other submissions. So what distinguished the play? The three aspects I just outlined above.

Meeting Professionals

Another way in which I benefited from the ATL internship was the ability to see live theatre in rehearsal. I saw rewrites taking shape on the stage, actors making adjustments, and shows going through trial and error. I also had the opportunity to work backstage, doing crew work, props, and even occasional "walk-ons" (I played a wordless jogger in a new Israel Horovitz play, and a dancing cake at the end of *Room Service*, which had an amazing cast including future playwright John Pielmeier and the legendary actor who was also the Artistic Director's father, Victor Jory).

But most importantly, I met living, breathing playwrights such as Beth Henley, John Guare, and Marsha Norman, who seemed to be fairly normal human beings (even though they had made the strange decision to write plays). They were all excited to be there, nervous about the process, and constantly thinking about how to improve their scripts. Little did I realize I was giving my arm to a future Pulitzer winner, as I helped Beth Henley across an icy parking lot to the theater.

The First Play

Meeting living writers, who were not Chekhov or Ibsen but had no hesitation to follow in their footsteps, I began to believe that being a playwright was perhaps not such an absurd goal. But I still lacked the courage and confidence to try it myself. That is, until Jon Jory himself came into the literary office out of the blue, sat down with me, and asked me if I ever thought about writing a play. Surprised and unprepared, I think I answered affirmatively, which is all he needed to hear. "We're doing an anthology of ten-minute plays for the apprentice company," he told me. "Why don't you try doing one of them?" Since I was evidently shocked into silence, he stood up to leave the room. Then he turned and added, "And we're holding a contest. One hundred dollars if you win."

Has anyone ever received bolder encouragement than that, at a young age? Being told to try something—why not?—and there might even be a little *money* in it? With that kick in the pants, I embarked on a new career. All because someone gave me a chance, without the slightest evidence that I deserved it. I would have been a fool to say no.

But I had to decide—*what* to write? I've always envied writers who wake up in the middle of the night with an idea that begs to be written. They put on a pot of coffee and get to it—sleep be damned. There are other writers who keep reams of notebooks with dozens of ideas for plays. Their biggest struggle is deciding which of their brilliant ideas to use first.

As for me, I get ideas all the time, and usually discard them just as quickly, as unusable or undramatic. But once in a while an idea will stick in my craw, and I can't shake it loose. That's the one I begin to pay attention to.

Do you have an idea for a story, an interesting character or two, or a situation involving those characters? More importantly, does that idea keep nagging at you over a period of days or weeks? That's an idea that's begging to be written.

My own idea resulted in a short play called *Changing of the Guard*, which allowed me to create characters based on a variety of personality types that I had known when I was in college, all of us cutting classes to watch the Watergate hearings. Irony became essential in this first play, and I've used it to some extent in every play since. So I guess you can say an identifying style was introduced as well.

What literary or theatrical techniques are you compelled to use in your first writings? A special tone, style, or point of view? More importantly, once you can identify it, can you begin to understand why it is so important to you? Chances are, if you can begin to realize the impulses that compel you to write like that, you'll begin to develop your individual "Voice."

As for my own first short play, the audience responded enthusiastically, and I did indeed win the prize money. That was my first payment for something I had written, and to this day, that hundred dollars meant more to me than any financial rewards ever since. It validated my new choice of profession. This was the point when I unashamedly admitted to myself (and maybe a few others), "I'm a playwright."

The First Full-Length Play

For my first attempt at a full-length play, I found myself intimidated by the prospect of an original story, so I tried my hand at an adaptation of a classic book in the public domain (meaning the rights are free and available to anyone who wants to use it). I readily admit that this was a somewhat timid move on my part, but I needed the practice of turning prose into dramatic writing. It was a bit like the exercise often recommended for writer's block: pick up a book, any book, and start typing it. Eventually you'll get so sick of the exercise that you'll enjoy the prospect of writing your *own* material.

My project was slightly more worthwhile than that, however. I had recently read *The Autobiography of Benvenuto Cellini*, an ancient text written by a bisexual sculptor and goldsmith from the sixteenth century, a book filled with excitement, outrageous bragging, ridiculous lies, and humor. In the tradition of some of the historical, epic plays I was fond of back then (*The Lion in Winter*, *Becket*, etc.), I thought that this would make an equally wonderful play, which I named *The Florentine*. I'm sorry to report that I was wrong about how wonderful it would be. But hey, it was my first try at a full length. And this was way before the invention of the internet, so I was also unaware that I wasn't the first to use Cellini's autobiography for literary inspiration: Ira Gershwin and Kurt Weill had already turned it into a Broadway musical, and Hector Berlioz had already turned it into an opera.[3] Without knowing better, I blindly decided this would be my entry into the world of full-length drama.

---

[3] John Patrick Shanley finally wrote another stage adaptation in 2002, called *Cellini*, which was produced at Second Stage in New York.

I brought out my typewriter, set up a piece of plywood on two sawhorses, sat on a broken desk chair that I had found on a street in Hell's Kitchen (that's where I got most of my furniture in those days), and started pounding it out. Days turned into weeks, and weeks into months, before I had finished a full draft of the adaptation. Then I picked it up and read it. Doubts began to form in my mind. As well as many disturbing questions. Was this a play that the American theatre would leap to produce? By now I had seen enough professional theatre to realize that large casts were prohibitive, and mine was enormous. It contained battle scenes, dozens of period costumes, and unnaturally literary dialogue. Cellini was a wonderful character, but none of the others were fascinating in their own right. Worst of all, my play (like the book) was extremely episodic.

In short, I realized I had written a very difficult, very expensive dud of a play. Ouch. Another person might have torn up the typewritten pages and head for the nearest bar. I decided to write something else.

It didn't take long for that next play to "break through" and garner national attention. It achieved acclaim, won awards, and brought me movie offers as well as an agent.

But it didn't happen quite as quickly as I make it sound. That play went through a period of *development*—one of the most controversial issues in American playwriting. I'll address that issue two chapters from now. But first, I had to figure out how and where to *submit* the new script. So let's address that topic next.

Points to Remember

- It's important to understand *why* you want to write a particular play.

- A good idea doesn't equal a story.

- Before you start writing, you'll probably need to have at least some idea of the beginning, the middle, and the end of your play. Also, how the characters change (or "arc") between the beginning and the end.

- Keep in mind that things can change as you write (and often do). Not only is that okay, but it's also probably a good sign. Don't discard those impulses—pay attention.

- Playwright training can be done in six ways: 1. College and Graduate Programs, dedicated to the art of Dramatic Writing, 2. Low-Residency Programs, 3. Online and Extension Programs, 4. Internships at professional theaters that specialize in New Play Programs, 5. Playwrights' Groups and Associations, and 6. Self-taught, meaning you should read and see as many plays as you can!

- How do you get your play noticed, among all the hundreds of others being submitted to theaters or competitions? Strong conflict, dialogue and characters, presented in an original way. Those factors are more crucial to the impact of a dramatic work than any theme or idea, no matter how powerful they may be.

- It's important to be prepared for sudden opportunities when they land in your lap. It's not up to you to consider the timing. Be *cautiously* prepared to say "yes!"

- Pay attention to an idea that just won't go away, and think about the reasons you're compelled to use it. Also, be aware of any special techniques you're drawn to, whether they involve tone, style, or point of view.

- When writing about historical subjects, or adapting material from previous sources, do a little research to see if someone else has already accomplished what you're trying to do. Be aware of their previous success or failure, then determine if you should proceed.

- Every writer has written something, or will write something, that he or she realizes doesn't work before it ever sees the light of day. When this happens to you, use it as a learning experience. When and how did you come to the realization that you were wrong? How can you use the lesson of this error to prevent similar mistakes in the future?

3 Submissions

What Are Plays Supposed to Look Like?

By the way, the only reason I knew what plays were supposed to look like was the fact that I had been required to read hundreds of them beforehand. You may not have that opportunity (though I recommend it), and yet before you write, you will need to know something about standardized playwriting.

It's important that your plays look professional, even (or especially) if you're just starting out. !

You always want literary managers, producing theaters, actors, and directors to think you know what you're doing. Thus the importance of *looking* like you know what you're doing.

Many beginning playwrights attempt to copy the script formats they find in published scripts—something like this:

Bill: How does this look? (*MARY reads his script.*)

Mary: I guess it looks okay, at least that's the way it looks in the plays I've read.

But Mary is wrong. Printed versions of plays format dialogue like this in order to save on paper—less white space between the sentences. Whether you're submitting your plays on paper or online PDFs, most theatre professionals would appreciate it if your scripts use standardized script formatting—more like this:

BILL

Is this better?

MARY takes another look.

MARY

You know, it kinda does! Somehow, it looks more professional.

As you can immediately see, that takes up twice as much space on the page. Bad for the trees, perhaps, but actors and directors will thank you for giving them a script they can read better in rehearsal and have more room to scribble on. Literary managers and theatre producers will think, "Ah! An experienced playwright!" So you should use the standardized format whenever possible. Within those boundaries, feel free to experiment and play around with dialogue breaks and spacing; some contemporary playwrights do just that, with interesting results (Terrell Alvin McRaney and Suzan-Lori Parks come immediately to mind).

For more precise and detailed descriptions of playwriting, the DGA has provided examples of "Modern" and "Traditional" formats, which you can find online.[1] As the title suggests, the "Modern" version is more prevalent, but they are very similar and either is fine to use.

How the Heck Can You Get Someone to Read Your Play?

Short answer: you can't. If they don't want to read it, they won't. And it's a more brutal environment for new scripts than ever before. Many theaters have proudly announced that they no longer read plays, or take submissions—even from agents, or with recommendations. Their attitude can be paraphrased into the following: "If we haven't heard of you, we're not interested." Many famous writers who submitted their first plays blind—Tennessee Williams, for example—would never have a chance in today's theatrical environment.

---

[1] https://www.dramatistsguild.com/media/PDFs/modernformat.pdf and https://www.dramatistsguild.com/media/PDFs/traditionalformat.pdf

Submission

The very word harbors negative connotations, doesn't it? It conjures images of playwrights groveling on the ground, begging someone—anyone—to please read their plays. "Submit, you worm!" And that's an accurate reflection of how it can feel to beginning playwrights. It can be a frustrating and seemingly pointless process.

It also used to be quite expensive. Playwrights would have to copy their scripts, bind them, and mail them out to theaters and contests, with little hope of return. Thankfully, email submissions have made this a cheaper activity, with the exception of some major competitions that still require hard copies (as well as submission fees). You'll need to do your own research to decide whether it's worth it. For example, the Eugene O'Neill National Playwrights Conference charges a fee for their online application. You can argue about the ethics of charging fees to enter many competitions, but most playwrights are willing to pay the O'Neill for the remote chance of being selected for the most important playwrights' showcase in the country. On the other hand, paying fifteen dollars to a theatre competition you've never heard of might *seem* to reduce the odds—but it may be just as likely that they are using this contest as a money maker for their organization.

So how do you decide? Let me repeat the harsh truth.

No one *wants* to read your play.   **!**

Literary managers (who are in dwindling numbers) may have to, as part of their jobs, but artistic directors at theaters generally approach a stack of manuscripts with dread. I knew one artistic director who flew across the country to see a staged reading of one of my plays at a reputable play festival. He expressed enthusiasm for the reading, and asked if he could get a copy of the script. I informed him that I had sent it to him eight months earlier. Oops.

To be fair, many theaters can be overwhelmed with submissions, without the staff or financial resources to read them in a timely fashion (or at all). This is why most of the large ones (and many of the smaller ones) have put restrictions on what scripts they will accept for consideration. They may accept agent submissions only. They may only look at plays recommended to them by a theatre professional. Or, as I mentioned, an increasing number of theaters will say they no longer accept submissions at all. Some theaters will try to be slightly more inviting to local playwrights, by only accepting scripts submitted from their immediate geographical regions. And some will allow you to submit the first ten pages and a synopsis. But play submissions can often be exercises in frustration.

Agents

What about landing an agent? It's a classic "catch-22" situation: they're usually not interested until you have a major production, and it's hard to get a major production without an agent. It's all about their ability to *sell* your work—and if there's not yet any interest in your work, they can't sell it. Truth is, you're probably going to be more effective selling it yourself.

There's a famous scene from the movie *Tootsie* (written by two Broadway playwrights, Larry Gelbart and Murray Schisgal) which is all about the function of a theatrical agent. Michael Dorsey (played by Dustin Hoffman), an angry struggling actor, goes to visit his agent George (played by Sydney Pollack). Michael's agent hilariously makes it clear that it's not his function to *find jobs* for his clients, but to field *offers*—and Michael doesn't have any.[2] It's pretty much the same with

---

[2]Larry Gelbart and Murray Schisgal (1982), *Tootsie*: N.p.: n.p. Print.

playwrights who have agents. You're still on your own—at least until there's some clamor to produce a play you've written.

Happily, there is some good news for playwrights! There are some notably successful attempts to get theaters to actually find new plays. One of the most proactive organizations in America is the National New Play Network,[3] run by Nan Barnett (whom I interviewed for this book). This is an organization in service to theaters that commit to producing new work. Not only that, but they also agree to be one of several theaters that will simultaneously produce a "rolling premiere." This commitment represents a conscious attempt to combat the previously common phenomenon of "premieritis"—an affliction I've known all too well as a playwright.

"Premieritis"

This was, and to some extent still is, a long-standing and commonly used practice, which hurts the playwright at the expense of a perceived advantage to theatrical institutions. Most theaters insist on the *exclusive* right to premiere a play. Part of the reason is for the special allure attached to the word "premiere." There is a commonly held belief that there is a marketing advantage in being the first theater to introduce a new play. This can break down to absurd levels: a production may be called a World Premiere, East Coast or West Coast Premiere, Regional Premiere, or even a Local Premiere (I keep expecting the first Neighborhood Premiere).

The so-called buzz of a "premiere" is terrific when landing a first production, but it also causes reluctance when trying to interest theaters in second or third productions—there's less incentive for the theaters. This is a definite disadvantage for the

---

[3] www.nnpn.org

playwright, and one that I encountered over and over in my own experience.

The word "premiere" seems to have its own kind of magic, though I've never thought this translates into any kind of meaning to ordinary audiences. Let's be frank. The people who buy the tickets usually care about two things—what it's about and who's in it. Who wrote it, or who produced it first, makes little difference to them.

The National New Play Network

Fortunately, Nan Barnett—and the 110 theaters in 70 American cities that comprise the membership of the National New Play Network (NNPN)—agree about the dissipating importance of premiering a play. Nan believes "premieritis" is "a leftover term from the 1990s,"[4] and she certainly gives evidence that she may be right. Member theaters commit to producing a single play three times within a year, and the NNPN provides financial support. In addition, NNPN offers further financial support in the form of residencies, commissions, and workshops at its member theaters. The numbers are impressive. Since its founding in 1998, there have been over 200 productions of 61 plays (at the time of this writing), and over 800 subsequent productions. So the rolling premieres are creating their own buzz and leading to plays that get frequent productions.

As I said, this is a service organization for theaters, not playwrights. Playwrights cannot apply directly to the NNPN. But Nan emphasizes there are two ways for playwrights to take advantage of her organization.

First, ingratiate yourself with member theaters. Many of them will not accept submissions, so it's important to do some

---

[4]Interview with the author, September 14, 2016.

research, see which ones produce plays that are similar to your style and content, and write them a query letter to see if they'd be interested. And by all means start hanging out at the member theaters near you, seeing their shows, attending their talk backs and receptions, and talking to their literary staff whenever possible. Make yourself *known*. As Nan said to me in a fun, tongue-twisting way, "The networking part of the network is what makes the network work." And keep in mind that these are all theaters that are actively searching for new plays to produce!

The New Play Exchange

Which brings me to Nan's second suggestion for playwrights who want to reach out to NNPN theaters: join the New Play Exchange (NPX).[5] This is a website designed to serve playwrights, administered by NNPN under the leadership of Gwydion Suilebhan. The NPX (as he designates the acronym) is an online clearinghouse of plays and playwrights, a single site where theaters, directors, and literary managers can search for new plays by subject matter or cast size, and where playwrights can read each other's work and recommend them to interested parties. Playwrights are invited to post their scripts online, either in full or in part, as well as describe them and provide the development history. At the time of this writing, the database is approaching 10,000 plays.

That may seem like a daunting number, but keep in mind that the 110 theaters (and growing) in the NNPN are actively searching for new plays—and they receive *free access* to all the scripts on the NPX. It's also important to remember that the purpose of the NPX is to allow theaters to search and find the precise *kinds* of plays they are looking for. This is where the most crucial feature

---

[5]https://newplayexchange.org

of the site comes into play—*tagging*. A playwright is asked to provide search terms for their plays, so a theater can find their work more easily. Examples such as "ecology," "drug addiction," "comedy," "African American," "Pennsylvania," or "female cast" can help a theater narrow down the choices for a play that suits their agendas or needs, straight to your script.

In 2016, when I asked Gwydion if he had any statistics regarding the relative "success" of the website, he understandably responded:

> I'm really reluctant to give you any stats about the NPX for one reason: they get very quickly out of date, thanks to how popular the platform is. Any number I gave you right now—say, the number of playwrights or the number of plays—would be out of date in a significant way by, say, a month from now, let alone a year. We have 40% more playwrights today than we did one year ago, for example, and 70% more theaters.
>
> At the end of the day, there are still about 25,000 playwrights in North America and 2,500 world premiere production slots in a given year. . . . Trying to change that fact might be a noble goal, but it's not the goal of the NPX.
>
> What we ARE doing, we think, is making the process by which those 2,500 world premieres are selected more human, more open, more transparent, and more egalitarian. Now that submissions are officially dead or dying—now that the submission paradigm has become so distasteful and broken and universally dreaded—we find that the new sharing-and-discovery model established by the NPX resonates with people. No longer do those 25,000 playwrights need to work so desperately to get their plays here and there in front of this or that person, to prepare exactly the right packet of materials. They can simply post their work on the NPX where anyone can find it and that's that.[6]

---

[6]Gwydion Suilebhan (2016), email.

The partnership of the NNPN and the NPX may be the most encouraging news I can provide for the readers of this book. The NPX has writers who've posted their plays from more than 40 countries, and international exchange programs as well, so this should be of global interest to playwrights everywhere.

Other Submission Methods

There are also several other efforts to promote specific groups of playwrights, such as the recent efforts to promote awareness of female writers by organizations such as The Kilroys, Los Angeles Female Playwrights Initiative, and Guerrilla Girls.

It's clear that all these special groups became necessary due to the difficulty of playwrights who want to get noticed. On the other hand, believe it or not, there are still many theaters—usually smaller or "fringe" companies—which actively seek and invite new play submissions. I've learned how to pick and choose, and you should also avoid the temptation to devour the submission opportunity lists and send your plays to as many as you can. You might get results from the sheer *volume* of your output, but play submission shouldn't be like playing the lottery.

For heaven's sake, do some research.

If a theater requires agent submission, don't bother with it for now. Nor should you bombard theatrical agents with query letters—that will get you nowhere. Try to get your play produced somewhere else, on your own. Once you are produced, agents will take more interest in you, and one of them may help you gain access to the larger theaters.

Focus on the theaters that express interest in unknown writers— and yes, there are some. Figure out which theaters produce plays that match the kind of plays you like, and the kind of plays you write. Also, since smaller companies don't have the budgets to bring in nationally based playwrights for residency during rehearsals, they are often more interested in producing local writers. So seek out those companies that are closer to home and get to know them.

Self-production

Another method, which is becoming more popular every year, is simply to stop waiting for other people to take notice, and produce your plays yourself. After decades of frowning on this practice, the DGA is now advocating that solution (partly to increase the ranks of their membership, but also to encourage the beginning playwright against the difficult odds of securing professional productions).

Playwrights have formed several organizations to produce their own work, including 13P in New York (now disbanded), The Workhaus Collective in Minneapolis, the Tremblors in Los Angeles, and The Welders in Washington, DC. These are often temporary organizations that go through a single cycle of self-production.

Other playwrights secure the funding to produce their own plays through other means. Online "crowdfunding sites" such as Kickstarter, Indiegogo, or GoFundMe have had major impacts on how to raise money for projects. Or—and this is always a major risk—pull out the credit card and pay for it yourself. In Mel Brooks's film *The Producers*, Max Bialystock tells Leo Bloom the most important rule of producing: don't ever put your own money in the show.[7] But it's not necessarily true. It could be hard to convince others to invest when you won't take a small risk yourself. It might be helpful to get the pot started with a little "seed money" out of your own pocket. And if the show is

---

[7]*The Producers*. Dir. Mel Brooks. 1968.

critically and financially successful, next time you won't have to convince anyone—theaters will come to *you*.

Let's now list the ways you can get your scripts read:

1 **Theaters**. As we've pointed out, it's increasingly unlikely that you can send your scripts to a producing theater and actually get it read. This is where networking becomes important again. If you actually make it a point to meet with the literary staff of a theater, and attend events related to new play development, those folks will have an easier time connecting your face to the play you've written—and that's definitely an advantage. Do try and get involved with the theaters closer to your home, which will usually have a commitment to respond to artists in their own community (thus the geographical exception for many submission restrictions).

2 **Play Competitions and Conferences.** In my opinion, these are still the best ways for fledgling playwrights to get their plays seen and discussed. My students have had terrific success landing slots at these events around the country, which have sometimes resulted in full productions of their work. That's how I started, too, as I will describe in the next chapter.

3 **Getting to Know Directors.** Not only do artistic directors select seasons for their theaters, but freelance directors are often in a position to bring scripts to theaters who want to work with them. The director-playwright relationship is often crucial to both of their careers. So try to form an ongoing association with a director who "gets" your work, and time will often take care of the rest.

4 **Service Organizations.** Playwrights' groups will promote new readings, and websites such as the NPX will provide opportunity to access the scripts online.

The NNPN is composed of theaters who are willing to co-produce new plays so that playwrights achieve more visibility.

5 **Self-production.** Increasingly beneficial (although sometimes done at financial loss), this gives a playwright the ability to have a show in production, and invite critics and other producing theaters to take a look. It is also an invaluable learning experience.

In terms of sending your scripts out, by snail mail or email, how can you tell which opportunities are worthwhile? Most of the ongoing American contests and competitions may be found in *The Dramatists Guild Resource Directory*, which may be accessed by Dramatist Guild members on the DGA website. This is an essential resource for any playwright—one that lists theaters, contests, and competitions accepting new plays, how and when to submit them, developmental programs, grants and fellowships, and many more opportunities for playwrights at any level of experience.

Points to Remember

- Proper, standardized play formatting gives you the advantage of looking like a professional playwright.

- Very few theaters and artistic directors want to read your play. Your purpose is to beat the odds.

- There are many ways of getting around the "agent submissions only" requirement. Remember that agents are not particularly helpful in landing productions, anyway—they are there to "field offers" (as explained in the movie *Tootsie*) and to represent you when you have an actual contract.

- Ways of getting your script read include: 1. networking onsite with theaters near you, 2. play competitions, festivals, and conferences, 3. developing professional associations with directors, 4. advocacy groups and social media sites, and 5. self-production.

- An essential tool for any American playwright submitting work is the *Dramatists Guild Resource Directory*.

4 Developing Your First Play

What If Your Play Isn't Perfect?

Guess what? Then your play is as imperfect as every other play, no matter which award-winning writer or fledgling beginner wrote it. There's no such thing as a perfect play. There's no such thing as a perfect *anything*, if you haven't realized that yet. All you can hope is that you get close.

Your first draft probably should only be about writing what you *want* to write. Therefore, it should be fun (but rarely is). Just remember, you don't *have* to think about the flaws in your writing—at least not while you're writing the first version. Okay, I just lied again. It's unavoidable to recognize problems while you're in the midst of writing your first draft—but don't let them deter you. Just keep on writing, understanding you'll have plenty of chances to fix those problems later. Don't get distracted. Keep at it until you write those magic words: "End of Play." Breathe deeply. Get some exercise. Celebrate in whatever way feels appropriate to you. Finally, get some long overdue and well-deserved sleep. Because when you wake up the next day, the real work begins. Yikes.

Unfortunately for writers of all kinds, there comes a day when like it or not, you'll have to actually show someone what you've been working on for the last several weeks, months, or years. It's a moment of courage for anyone who wants to present themselves as a writer, and I've seen plenty of them crumble in the process. But you must have a certain amount of confidence in your work to show it—as well as a necessary amount of flexibility to be willing to amend it.

And this is the difficult truth: once you show your finished play to someone who matters, they will most likely tell you it *isn't* finished.

This is a usual part of the process in getting your play produced—you have to take it through the sometimes helpful, often painful ritual of *development*. It's a rare occasion indeed when any playwright can submit a play to a director or producer and hear that it's perfect as it stands, and will be produced without delay. Instead, they will tell you it needs "work."

And if you're human, as I assume you are, that can hurt. I've often wished I were a visual artist instead, who can display their achievement and receive a clearly interpreted thumbs up or thumbs down. I don't think anyone told Rembrandt or even Andy Warhol, "It shows a lot of promise but still needs something. Keep working on it and show it to us when it's a little further along."

On the other hand—I will now incite fury among some of my peers—I'm here to tell you that when it comes to dramatic writing, they're right to say so. Here's a famous quote, usually attributed to Ernest Hemingway: "The first draft of anything is shit." Most professional writers would tend to agree with that. And first drafts of plays are especially prone to such criticism—especially the draft that is written *before* it's handed to actors. Because it's almost always true that playwrights don't know exactly what they've got until they hear their work out loud. And that's exactly what your play needs at this stage.

How Do You Organize a Cold Reading?

Most beginning playwrights are stunned by their first experiences with actors reading the roles in their plays. A frequent response is one of shock—"I never thought it would sound like that." That's the best realization you can have.

It's important to listen to experienced actors, who are doing their best to interpret the material on the page. ❗

They may be unsure, confused, or downright baffled by the characters as they read their roles. They may also be excited and energized, possibly giving the language wonderful nuances and meanings that you, the playwright, never imagined. The actors will tell you—by their interpretations—what you've written, and how much or how little further work is going to be required. They will tell you the dramatic potential of your play. To tell the truth, the ability to do cold readings is one of the most essential tools any contemporary actor should possess.

The cold reading is the most useful thing a playwright can arrange after writing a first draft. ❗

Gather some actor friends, or even playwright and director friends who can sort of act, and have them read your play out loud. Provide refreshments (no booze till afterwards—play it safe), and make it a casual occasion. Try to relax, so they will feel relaxed too. Don't give them long character descriptions beforehand. Don't ask them to try accents, dialects, or affected voices. The only thing you might want to provide beforehand is pronunciation of difficult words, if any. Most importantly, don't tell them the intended tones, rhythms, volumes, or effects; don't even mention whether it's a comedy or a drama. Let them discover those things on their own—as you will yourself.

Appoint someone to read stage directions—this should not be done by you, and it should probably not be done by someone without stage experience. Explain that there are stage directions that don't need to be read, since the actors can play the moments themselves without help: "Pause," "She becomes angry," "He hums to himself," etc.

Now everyone should be ready. Just let the actors read the play—without interjection, without suggestion, without comment. Your job is to sit there and listen. Listen well. Listen for the segments of your play that seem static or stuck, listen for sections that are likely missing and cause confusion or uncertainty in their absence, listen for the parts that fly like the wind and make the actors shift into first gear. Although you may be too reluctant or nervous to tear your eyes away from the page, look up from the script now and then, and watch the actors' faces. Tears, smiles, frowns, and yawns are all very telling signs about to what extent they're understanding your play. So pay attention—don't withdraw and pull into yourself. Be present and aware.

When the reading is over, be sure to thank them for their efforts. For God's sake, don't tell them they read it wrong! They are using the best information available to them to interpret your play correctly—your *script*, as you wrote it. So if someone goes in an unexpected direction, use their reading as an instructive tool. Don't be upset if it sounds a bit different from the way you imagined. That happens all the time, and it's usually a very good thing. You may hear tonal choices and intonations that do a better job of bringing the characters to life. On the other hand, if one of the actors interprets his or her role in a way that damages your intended purpose, it's a strong signal to you that you will need to rewrite that part with more clarity and definition.

As I said, your primary job at a reading is to *listen*. And if you listen well to your play as it is being read, you will have plenty of fodder to prepare yourself to write the next draft. ❗

Now comes the hard part. Do you ask for further feedback from the participants? It's a tricky business. In my experience, most invitations for the actors, directors, and other attendees to respond after a reading usually result in an immediately uncomfortable pause—not necessarily because they don't know what to say, but more often because they are reluctant to give opinions that may unintentionally offend or hurt the playwright. After all, it's in the very nature of good actors that they learn *empathy*—so they can sense the potential danger in an unwelcome response.

You can help them out, by being friendly and welcoming, and by asking specific questions about your play. Not "What did you think?" or "Did you like it?"—which are useless questions without helpful answers. Instead, ask questions that truly pertain to what you just heard, and how they chose to interpret your material: "Do you think your character is consistent in that scene?," "Does the dialogue in Scene Four make sense, or are you confused?," or even "How does the ending make you feel?," if you can't tell from the reading itself. If any such questions as these arose as you listened, feel free to ask them now. It gives the actors the sense that their reading had some beneficial impact, and that's a nice way to end the session.

On the other hand, be careful about asking for suggestions to "fix" the play, or ways to make it "better." Such vague entreaties can result in a very confused discussion with many different solutions.

Most importantly, keep this post-reading feedback session *short*—I would advise a half-hour maximum. Then make it clear it's over, and break out the beer and munchies. There may be one or two people who aren't quite done talking about the play; it's better that they do that privately with you, so you can politely nod and tell them you'll give their extra feedback some thought (whether you will or not). Then offer them some wine and cheese. Because chances are you've already heard most everything you need, from the reading itself.

The first reading—done in private, with friends and peers—is the easiest and most valuable way to actually understand what the heck you may have written. Unfortunately, unless one of those folks happens to be a commercial producer or an artistic director at a theater, that reading is unlikely to engender an actual production. So there are other opportunities for play development that can serve as a "showcase" for your play, displaying it for potential "buyers."

Are There Other Ways to Develop New Scripts?

Okay. This is where the *real* controversy about new play development lies—in institutionally sponsored competitions that result in staged readings for certain audiences. These are some of the most sought after opportunities in American theatre—but to some playwrights, based on their personal experiences, also the most reviled. This is where the phrase "Developed to Death" raises its ugly head. The suspicion is that a play may be selected for "development" (which could mean anything from a private reading to a full workshop ending with a public performance, depending on the institution), only to fulfill the private agendas of the sponsoring organization.

What agendas? Well, grants are often a big reason that theaters do new play development. Most American regional theaters have non-profit status, and rely largely on grants for operating expenses. Showing that their theaters have programs that develop new plays will automatically generate more grant money, since they have evidence that they're interested in new work . . . even though their actual productions may usually reflect older, more traditional tastes. The result of this common predicament is that playwrights often feel they receive "token" development.

Developmental Programs

There are also reputable programs that are devoted to the playwright being able to develop his or her work in private, without the pressures of pleasing producers. The National Playwrights Conference at the Eugene O'Neill Center in Connecticut is the granddaddy of these programs (with well over a thousand plays submitted a year), but I'll list others toward the end of this chapter. Playwrights that I have known have had widely varying experiences in such programs: some responses have been ecstatic and career-changing; some have been bitter and painful.

I once attended a public reading of a new play by a very famous female playwright. In the talkback session after the reading, an audience member gave her what I immediately recognized as an unhelpful comment. The playwright responded, "That's the worst idea I've ever heard. I wouldn't do that in a million years."

Ouch! On the one hand, good for the playwright to have the guts and self-confidence to say something like that. On the other hand, I think it's generally best to respond with a smile, a thanks for the comment, and the offer to consider that suggestion in the future—which is of course a lie, but a kinder, gentler way to deal with someone who is trying to be supportive, however awkwardly. By all means listen with a friendly, generous attitude to each and every comment, and keep your ears open for an unexpected gem of wisdom from an unlikely source—believe me, those do occasionally happen!

Keep in mind that in terms of the effectiveness of any program, there are a lot of factors at work, including the temperament of the playwright, the personalities of whoever may be on staff during a particular season, and the resources to develop a play in the right way. Some plays require a lot of rewriting during the course of development, which is why the best programs have an introductory session a month or two before the actual workshop. That allows the playwright to hear the work early enough to make substantial changes before the workshop commences. The catch, of course, is that the final script may be substantially different from the play that was originally chosen. This sometimes tends to alarm the people that picked the play in the first place (though it shouldn't).

Although most of my experiences with playwrights' conferences have been wonderful, I had a difficult time at one (it shall remain nameless, although my discretion doesn't matter since it quickly went defunct). After one day of trying to work on my script, I realized that it would be impossible to do any rewriting there. The director was taking all his time trying to perfect the performance itself, treating it like a full production even though the end result was a staged reading. In short, he was trying to show off, and garner attention for himself as a flashy director, instead of providing a good showcase for a new play. Frankly, the play itself didn't seem to matter, at least to him. So it was a waste of time as far as I was concerned. Fortunately, I had been selected for one other excellent conference that same summer, and was able to develop the play very well there.

I also witnessed another playwright's frustration at a different conference, where I myself was happily being treated well. In his case, the actors had so much input into the script that he spent each and every day rewriting his play to suit their whims. After two weeks, he threw away every subsequent draft and returned to his first version.

Two playwrights have been famously critical of developmental programs, and their cautions are worth mentioning here. The late Edward Albee was skeptical about the whole process: "It is to de-ball the plays; to castrate them; to smooth down all the rough edges so they can't cut, can't hurt. It's to make them commercially tolerable to a smug audience. It's not to make plays any better. Most playwrights who write a good play write it from the beginning."[1] Well, I can only speak for myself as a lesser

---

[1] Steven Samuels. "Interview with Edward Albee." *American Theatre*, September 1, 1994: n. pag. Web.

playwright, but I usually need time and resources to develop a first draft.

Another dissenting opinion is from Richard Nelson, who was chair of the Playwriting Program at Yale Drama School when he gave the keynote speech for the Alliance of Resident Theaters in 2007, and decried the infantilization of American playwrights, depicted by theatrical institutions as people who need "help" with their writing.[2] Nelson stirred up a lot of trouble that year, and many theaters and developmental programs reevaluated their methods. As a result, ten years later . . . little has changed.

As you can see, it's very hard to generalize about new play development. It can be a godsend or a hindrance, depending on the specific circumstances of the program you're invited to attend.

Despite the cautions above, I am generally a firm believer in developmental programs. The whole point of these programs is to give you an opportunity to hear your play, not with the goal of getting it produced (not yet, anyway), but with the intent to do further work on it.

By their very nature, these programs acknowledge the collaborative nature of playwriting, and the importance of developing your writing with the helpful elements of gifted actors, directors, and dramaturgs. Every early draft needs such attention, and most every experienced playwright understands the importance of these tools. From my own experiences and observations, I think most of these programs do an outstanding job.

My First Play Conference

My first experience with a developmental program led to the production of my first play. At the time, the Midwest Playwrights'

---

[2] Richard Nelson. "Thanks but No Thanks," *The American Theatre Reader*, 339–44. New York, NY: Theatre Communications Group, 2009. Print.

Program (a precursor to the current PlayLabs) was a program under the joint leadership of the Playwrights' Center in Minneapolis, and Dale Wasserman, best known for the stage adaptation of *One Flew Over the Cuckoo's Nest*, and the book for the musical *Man of La Mancha*. The Playwrights' Center paid my way to Minnesota, where I found myself ensconced in a summer camp along with the other selected playwrights, directors, and dramaturgs.

As you may remember, I had given up on my first attempt at playwriting, *The Florentine*. For my second effort, I went in the opposite direction—a three-character play with a unit set, which I described as "a comedy about divorce, suicide and farm maintenance." This play was by no means based on anything I had ever read, instead drawing inspiration from my own experience as a young person with an early failed marriage, trying to get his life together. The result was a modest work called *Losing It* (no relation to the Tom Cruise movie that was released a couple of years later). I wrote this one in ten days. It poured out of me without much effort.

I had read somewhere, possibly in *American Theater Magazine*, about a conference to develop new plays in Minnesota. So I submitted my play; months later, that submission secured me an invitation to Minnesota.

The procedure at Midwest Playwrights was a simple one—we all read our plays out loud, without the help of actors, and then received feedback from the group. Although I was a beginner, I was part of a group of accomplished writers, many of whom went on to major writing careers and university positions: Erik Brogger (now at Hofstra), Steven Dietz (now at UT Austin), Barbara Field (then a dramaturg at the Guthrie Theater), Charles Smith (now at Ohio University), and Laura Shamas (who went on to teach dramatic writing at USC and Pepperdine). This is a relatively undiscussed benefit of conference participation, by the way—*networking*.

Theatre is, as they say, a very small world. And you are bound to cross paths with people who will become important to you later on in life. There were also two young directors who would eventually become Tony Award winners on Broadway: Dan Sullivan, who directed my play in the conference, and Robert Falls, who chose my play for its first production at Wisdom Bridge Theater in Evanston.

In addition, Steven Dietz allowed me to crash on his couch when I moved to Minneapolis, and a few years later directed my most successful play, *T Bone N Weasel*. Barbara Field helped me to secure an agent. Charles Smith gave me a job one year as a visiting professor at Ohio University. And Laura Shamas became my wife—24 years later!

Right there you have one of the most important reasons to participate in developmental programs whenever you have the opportunity: you'll meet people. The importance of networking—however accidental or unintentional—can't be overstated here. No playwright can have any kind of progress without meeting people that have the power and influence to lend you support, help, and interest. Sometimes this can lead to full productions—if not by the people you meet directly, then by the people these folks may talk to.

What Tennessee Williams called "the kindness of strangers"[3] is a crucial aspect of surviving in the theatre. This profession can be harrowingly unpredictable, and that means you will have to rely on favors, kindnesses, and support from others. Be gracious enough to accept it, and know that you may find yourself in a situation when you should be offering similar help to others.

The theatre community is a family—a substitute for family for some, perhaps the *only* family for others—so it's important to

---

[3]Tennessee Williams. *A Streetcar Named Desire: A Play*. New York: New Directions, 1947. Print.

be familial with everyone who crosses your path. You will not, and cannot, have any true success as a playwright completely on your own. You will need others—and they will need you.

That means that you may have to go against your nature—as a solitary writer used to working alone—in order to put yourself out there and become known to theatre professionals. Don't be shy! Playwriting isn't just about writing plays—but how you get people to *learn* about your plays. Being a playwright involves three "P's," not just one:

a Playwriting
b Perseverance
c Promotion

The reading of my own play at Midwest Playwrights was received well: Dale Wasserman proclaimed (as my wife reminds me on a regular basis) "Not much to say about a play when it's that good."

Could I tell it read so well? Nope. I was the one doing the reading, so I couldn't really hear it. Did I know anything about play structure, characterization, or dialogue? Not really, other than what I had learned by reading and watching plays, especially at ATL. Keep in mind that I had never taken a playwriting class in my life. So this was all brand new to me. Due to my relative ignorance about playwriting, I simply wrote what I believed to be effective, without any evidence that it actually would be. That was kind of an advantage. I had no fear, nothing to lose. The specter of self-criticism was unknown to me (that would come later, of course), and I felt free to write any way I wanted.

We all went home for a month or so. Once everyone had dispersed and I was alone, I took a few days to fully digest what I learned. Then I tried to get ready for the next, most important step in developing my play—which by its very nature, I had to do on my own, without anyone helping me.

The Rewrite

Welcome to the second draft. As I said earlier—yikes. Now the *real* work begins. This is the point where, after a certain amount of work, you'll discover whether or not you have a play at all.

There are two groups of playwrights when it comes to rewriting. The first group is overjoyed to have finished the difficult first draft, and is anxious to put aside all the stress that accompanied those head-banging, finger-chewing late night sessions fueled by junk food and caffeine. Now to take that raw material and shape it into something, like a sculptor. They can't wait. I'm pleased to say I belong in this group.

The second group, however, is in a more difficult frame of mind. Those playwrights probably *enjoyed* writing that first draft (what is that like? I wish I knew!), and are reluctant to mess with whatever gave them pleasure the first time through. They may not really know how to begin—or they may resent having to do any further work at all. As you might guess, this group will have a much harder time with the rewrite process.

For heaven's sake, please don't kid yourself that your play doesn't require more work. That's impossible. You have a new goal now. Not only does your play need to please *you*, but now you also need to refine it so that it works for an *audience*. That's the whole point of the second draft (and third, and fourth, and tenth). Indeed, the old adage is true, so type this up and tape it to the wall in front of your laptop:

"Writing is Rewriting."

How to start rewriting? Well, let's first talk about what you probably *shouldn't* do. Or learn from your mistakes if you've already charged down the following destructive paths.

There are two common errors that I've witnessed (particularly from my own students) when it comes to rewriting:

a Throwing everything away and starting over. This is an emotional reaction that comes from the shock when you realize what you've written still seems to need further work. Push away any Frankensteinian impulse to destroy the monster you've created. That's a bit extreme. Instead, think about the readings you've heard, look over your notes from those sessions, and approach your text again in order to distinguish specific moments that work, from moments that don't work as well. That's called skillfully *editing*—as opposed to *replacing*—your writing.

b The other mistaken method is piling on more information, to make your writing more "clear"—more exposition, more explanation, more repetition. Nothing gets clearer, or more understandable, by overwriting. Indeed, the end result will probably result in more confusion than ever. Don't ignore the impulses that made you want to write a scene in the first place. *Embrace* that impulse, and simplify your text through dramatic action, driven by the characters' desires and conflicts.

Everything I learned from that first reading at the Midwest Playwrights Program, for better and worse, I incorporated into the next draft. By the time I finished, I was confident that the script was improved. I would not have been able to take it to the next step without hearing the actors read it. Eventually, over the subsequent days and months, I learned two things about rewriting that I've carried with me over my thirty-plus years in the theatre:

a Oddly, what seems to work on the page may not necessarily translate to the stage.

b Conversely, dialogue that may seem hesitant or uncertain as written may come alive in the process of rehearsal and performance.

Rewriting may sound like mental torture, but once you begin to do it, you should learn how to *enjoy* the painstaking process of making things better. In my opinion—believe it or not—this *is* the fun part! Not writing the first draft, which in my experience sometimes feels beyond any vision of Hell that Dante or Jean-Paul Sartre ever concocted. And certainly not Opening Night, when your job is essentially over and the play is in the hands of the actors. You don't even have to be there at that point (and sometimes you wish you weren't). But *development and rehearsal*—everything that comes in between—that will make it all worthwhile. Trust me.

The Staged Reading

After our month of rewriting, we reconvened at Lake Forest College in Illinois to meet our directors and to start blocking our plays, in preparation for public staged readings there and shortly thereafter at the Goodman Theater in Chicago. The rehearsal period was ten days.

Eventually, the intensity of those rehearsals (not just for my play, but for all the others too) became too much to handle. So a wild night of fighting with fire extinguisher foam was called for in the dormitories (don't tell anyone). Another night, a few of the writers and actors took time away from their own plays to write and perform impromptu sketches for their captive, but appreciative, audience.

Just as important as the time spent writing, rewriting, and in rehearsal, is the time spent *away* from the play altogether. !

Total immersion is not healthy; it's important to approach a play with a refreshed and renewed outlook, each and every single day. Sleepless nights don't often help—sleep does. Agonized, tortuous hours at the keyboard trying to solve dramaturgical puzzles don't help—but a hot shower or a long walk can, and often does.

Directors who have worked with me know that when I ask for a day away from rehearsals, it's because I've discovered an issue with the script, and need a bit of time to address it. If you have a director who gets nervous at such a suggestion, you're probably working with the wrong one. I usually return within a day with a major rewrite that improves the play significantly. With some experience and confidence, so will you.

Other than figuring out how to operate fire extinguishers, what did I learn during this rehearsal process? Plenty. Probably more than all of my previous theatre learning put together. I watched how my director, Dan Sullivan, worked with actors to physicalize language. "What are these people *doing*?" became an unexpectedly important question. A play is visual, not just words on a page. So we created stage action to accompany the dialogue. Sometimes the director contributed to these ideas, sometimes the actors, and occasionally they turned to me for possible ideas.

The final staged reading, held at the Goodman Theatre, was a triumph that led to my first production offer, from Bob Falls, for the world premiere at Wisdom Bridge Theater.

New play development can be informative and enjoyable, as it was for me in this case. But as I was to discover later, productions are for a paying audience—so the stakes are much higher. And the playwright is expected to knuckle down and *work*, all over again.

What Are the Leading Play Development Programs?

Before we get to the first production, I promised you that I would name some of the leading new play development programs. The best ones are naturally competitive (meaning quite hard to get into). They all attract a significant number of producing theaters looking for new scripts, whose artistic directors and literary managers attend on a regular basis. I'll start with the programs with which I've had personal experience:

a **The Eugene O'Neill Playwrights Conference**. Personal experience? Well, sort of. In the 1990s, I was selected for the conference with my play *Dimly Perceived Threats to the System*. Which *I turned down*. Suffice it to say I was an idiot; more about that later. At any rate, this is absolutely the hardest conference to get into; they usually get way over a thousand submissions, for approximately eight slots. But if chosen, you're working with folks at the top of their professions, and although critics are disallowed, theatre professionals from around the country attend this event religiously. This is the ultimate long shot worth taking.

b **The Sundance Institute Theatre Program**. Yes, Robert Redford is interested in developing plays as well as movies. I was there many years ago with *The Einstein Project*, a play I coauthored with Paul D'Andrea, and had the wonderful fortune to work with the late, great actor J. T. Walsh, who played Einstein. A terrific experience.

c **PlayLabs**, at the Playwrights' Center in Minneapolis. I had two plays developed there while a Core Member at the Playwrights' Center: *Fault Line*, which went on to a production in New Jersey, and *T Bone N Weasel*, which became my most popular play. You do have to be a Core Member of the Center to be eligible for consideration by PlayLabs, but I would also encourage submitting yourself for membership.

d **New York Stage and Film**, at Vassar College. This was another opportunity for me to develop *Dimly Perceived Threats to the System*, so it calmed a few of my deep regrets for turning down the O'Neill. A great showcase as well.

e **The Lark Play Development Center** in Manhattan. Although I have yet to secure a reading there personally, my wife and a few of my students have had wonderful readings there through various programs that target specific groups and levels of experience. This is an invaluable resource for new play development.

Friends and students have also participated in other prominent programs, such as Play Penn in Philadelphia, Seven Devils Playwrights Conference in Idaho, New Harmony Project in Indiana, Orlando Festival of New Plays, and Bay Area Playwrights Festival in the San Francisco area.

There are many websites that list such opportunities, including the excellent one maintained by the Playwrights' Center (a very good reason to become a paying member there is access to their opportunities list). And as I mentioned before, *The Dramatists Guild Resource Directory* is available on the DGA website with an exhaustive list of play contests, competitions, and many other resources for playwrights.

Many playwrights create submission calendars for themselves, so they won't forget the deadlines for the developmental opportunities that seem the most relevant and exciting for their own plays. Some playwrights even challenge themselves to submit a play a week. Still, learn something about each

and every organization before you blindly submit to them—
especially if they require application fees!

Points to Remember

- The easiest and most important thing you can do after writing your first draft is to arrange a cold reading.

- Your main job is to *listen*. Afterwards, if there's a discussion, ask specific questions based on what you heard during the reading. Don't ask for vague reactions.

- Organized new play development programs can be a godsend, but it depends upon various factors, including the level of talent and experience involved. Be careful not to relinquish your own authorial rights—but also try to be flexible and open to helpful suggestions. It's a tricky balance that can require some practice.

- Another useful aspect of play conferences is the chance to *network* with theatre professionals. This can lead to ongoing relationships with theaters, directors, and actors in the future. Shyness does not profit you in the theatre.

- The three P's—Playwriting, Perseverance, and Promotion—are essential skills for survival in the theatre.

- The rewriting process is an essential one, and it's important to approach it with eagerness, not resentment. Be careful about tossing all of your work away and starting over—that's rarely a good method. Nor should you approach rewriting by adding more and more exposition and explanation. Judicious editing is almost always what is needed when rewriting the first draft.

- Occasional time away from your script—during developmental rehearsals and writing time—will often give you fresh perspectives on the needs of the play. Ask for the time you need when you need it (with reason, of course).

- Regularly peruse play submission opportunities, through the various online resources as well as the *Dramatists Guild Resource Directory*. Many playwrights create a submission calendar for themselves, as a way of remembering deadlines for the opportunities that interest them the most.

5 Rehearsal and Production (If Things Go Well)

The Rehearsal Room

For some reason, a playwright in the rehearsal room can cause panic.

Not just for the writer, but often for the other people there, especially if they lack experience working on new plays. The first time in rehearsal can be a mystifying experience for beginning playwrights. Do they even belong there? Where do they sit? Are they allowed to talk? What do they say to the director and actors? Are they allowed to voice an opinion? Are they allowed to rewrite? And if so, for how long? Is it okay to leave? Most importantly, *how* do they express their needs and concerns?

In our program at Catholic University, we provide what I believe to be the most valuable aspect of professional training for young playwrights—we *produce* their plays. Not a staged reading, not a minimally designed presentation, but a full-blown professional quality production, directed by one of the leading directors in the theatrically rich Washington, DC theatre scene. And an important part of *my* job is to prepare them for what may happen in that rehearsal room. That's the main reason I decided to write this book—because of the importance of that training.

I'm going to continue to discuss the journey of my own first play, *Losing It*, since the roller coaster ride that it took me on represented nearly every precipitous climb and harrowing descent that any playwright can possibly experience. Today my award-winning introductory play is completely unknown, an obscure footnote without much lasting significance, other than it introduced me to the world of theatre. But in less than a year, I learned an enormous amount of valuable information about success and failure—information I was able to digest and apply the next time I was lucky enough to land another professional break, with much happier results. And much of what I learned— for good and for bad—happened in the rehearsal room.

Good Rehearsals

As I mentioned, around the time of the public presentation at the Goodman Theatre, Bob Falls told me he was interested in producing my play at Wisdom Bridge in Evanston. I also received a Jerome Fellowship, to allow me to be in residence for a year at the Playwrights' Center in Minneapolis. So I moved from New York to Minnesota.

Rehearsals for the production at Wisdom Bridge began a few months later, and I came to Evanston to be in residence from the very start. Up to this point, I had learned some things about rehearsal from the previous workshop (which I've described to you), but I quickly realized this would be different: a lot more rehearsals, a lot more questions about the meaning and intent of each and every moment in the play, and informative challenges from the director. Falls wanted to maintain the comedy of the piece, but he was equally concerned with truth and consistency; he encouraged me to cut any lines that seemed "writerly" (meaning a gag for gag's sake, or a line that showed off the author's cleverness rather than the illumination of character).

Falls, as a director who had plenty of experience developing new work, was very comfortable with me in the room. That made things very easy for me (I had no idea *how* easy until my second production). It was an open forum, where he could ask me questions in front of the actors, and I was invited to speak up whenever the actors had a question. Falls also had the advantage of already knowing how well the play could work in front of an audience (as did one of the actors, who reprised his role from the workshop), so that gave us all confidence. Rehearsals were playful, joyful experiences.

I also began to learn the normal protocol for communication in the room, which is that any *major* changes or suggestions should be sifted like flour into an orderly funnel—namely the director. I was certainly confident and welcome enough to speak to the actors about little things (inflections, minor word changes, simple line cuts). But any ideas for major textual rewrites, cuts, or character reconsiderations were to be addressed privately to the director first. Otherwise there would be flour all over the room! Then he *usually* let me explain what I wanted to change to the actors. That, of course, was assuming he was in agreement; if not, we spoke at length during the next break, so the actors wouldn't have to be subject to the anxiety-producing sight of a playwright seeming to argue with the director. There's nothing more destructive to a healthy rehearsal than arguing in front of others—it's impolite, confusing, and damaging to the health of the ensemble. It makes everyone else in the room wonder whether something is *wrong* with the show—even if there isn't!

I was invited to stay for the technical rehearsals, which I did before I understood my presence wasn't crucial. Technical rehearsals are the final, excruciatingly long days that occur right before the show opens to the public, when lighting, costumes, sound, scenery, and all the other design elements are introduced. The usual method is to slowly crawl through all the technical cues of the show—a "cue to cue"—and it can often take a half-hour to go through two pages of text. My show had a unit set, so most of the cues involved lights and sound. After a few hours, I asked if I was needed, and Falls grinned at me, saying "I'm surprised it took you this long to ask." I took a few days to explore Chicago and some of the other theatre happening around town, particularly this strange new ensemble performing out of a church basement (who called themselves "Steppenwolf").

The Production

I returned for previews, which became my favorite part of the whole process (and still is!). I quickly learned how to sit in the back of the house and gauge the responses from the audience: where they were delighted, where they were bored, where they were confused. And we all made adjustments each and every night after the performance, in order to try things a little differently the following night.

To this day, I'm thrilled when I get more than one preview to adjust the premiere of a new play—although sometimes I've been lucky to get just one.

There are four consecutive stages of learning about your play, in increasing order of importance:

1. The cold reading.
2. A workshop (if at all possible), scripts in hand.
3. Rehearsal for production.
4. Previews—the more the merrier.

You may have noticed I've left out the next step, which is the Opening Night. That's because a playwright's work is done by then—it all belongs to the actors from then on. There may be some value in returning halfway or toward the end of a run, having put some time and space between you and the play, and attempting to look at it again with fresh eyes—but only to make mental notes for what you hope will be a second (or third) production of the play.

I hope I've been able to convey the thrill of having your play produced. As I said early on, you won't make much money, and you probably won't become famous, but the sheer excitement of having your story told in front of an appreciative community is one of the greatest pleasures on earth. That's why I do it, that's why you want to do it, and let's face it, that's why there is such a proliferation of struggling playwrights today, despite the odds.

I remember when the late Elmore Leonard, an extraordinary novelist, announced that he wanted to write a play. I thought at the time that seemed like a perfect fit for someone who wrote such crackling dialogue, much of it ending up in remarkable movies like *Get Shorty, Out of Sight,* and *Hombre*. Yet he longed for the reaction of a live audience in a theater (this from a man who had over twenty films adapted from his novels!). Eventually he gave up this idea, because—and this is how I remember his quote—"Writing a play is hard." Yes, it is.

Working on my own first production, I learned about the true collaborative nature of theatre—to create living pictures that not only accompany, but also *illuminate* the text.

Everyone in the rehearsal room can be involved in the process—and more than that, they *should* be. **!**

The *script* remains yours, and yours alone. But the *play* is no longer yours—it belongs to everyone there. Making a play out of a script isn't just saying words out loud, just as building a house isn't just laying bricks, wood, and mortar on top of a blueprint. *Your* blueprint—the script—requires a team of people to turn it into something substantial, something sturdy—and hopefully, something remarkable.

What's It Like to Have a Hit?

The answer—it feels nice, but it can be a short-lived thrill. And that was the case with *Losing It,* which opened to rave reviews from both of the Chicago newspapers. It was Wisdom Bridge's bestselling show in a year or two, and the run was extended. Not only that, but it also won a national playwriting award, co-sponsored by the DGA and the CBS network. Among the judges for the award were John Guare and my idol, the man who had written *Moonchildren*, Michael Weller. Unfortunately, I didn't get to meet up with Weller when he arrived in Chicago to see my play. But I heard from Bob Falls that he made this comment: "Klein sure knows how to work a room." That might still be the favorite assessment of my work I've received to date.

On top of all this attention, I started getting enquiries from other theaters around the country. American regional theaters in the 1980s communicated with each other regularly, to find out which plays were popular with audiences. Thus many of them wanted to know if they could produce it too.

And they weren't the only folks enquiring—I started to receive letters from movie and television companies, either requesting to read my play or asking if I had any more. A friend of mine who was working in an entry-level position at a television studio in New York wrote me that she'd been hearing my play discussed all over town—by people who had never even seen it.

However, that success was short-lived—which brings me to the next chapter.

Points to Remember

- Talk to your director beforehand about rehearsal protocol. This can change from director to director, so it's important that you ask about your director's comfort with what you say, and when.

- Everyone in the rehearsal room can potentially be a source for making your play better. Keep your ears open!

- Ask to what extent you can use preview performances to make adjustments in the script. Depending on the number of previews, directors may have different opinions about late changes. But it doesn't hurt to ask!

- A hit show in one location may be a flop in the next. It doesn't necessarily have to do with the script; changes in cast, director, venue, and audience all have an impact. So expect your play to feel a bit different wherever it goes.

6 Rehearsal and Production (If Things *Don't* Go Well)

As I just stated, my first production was a rousing success. And . . . no one has heard of it since. Within a year, it died a horrible, excruciating death (the title became eerily ironic). Such is the life of a playwright (or at least it can be). Now I'll get into the details of what went wrong, so you can learn some of the lessons I learned the hard way.

How can you avoid a Flop? Well, if bad reviews and empty houses dictate that your show goes belly up, there's not much you can do but accept it and move on to the next project. However, poor decisions during contract negotiation, casting, and rehearsal may also be detrimental, and can often be avoided. These are all things playwrights should be aware of and prepare for in advance. Next I'll try to identify a few of these land mines . . . by recounting mistakes I made myself. Some of my mistakes had to do with poor decisions on my part, a lack of foresight, and a willingness to be produced under questionable circumstances. I'll discuss them in some detail now, so you may learn from my cautionary example.

Mistakes to Avoid

Losing It was a hit in Chicago, but its success crumbled when it left town. Why? I made a series of errors in judgment, and most of them involved relinquishing control to other people. I was still young, a kid who had little firsthand experience in professional theatre. I had one show to date, it was successful, and I naively thought that's how things would continue. I was setting myself up for a precipitous fall.

My first mistake was letting my agent (now deceased) decide the next step for me; I thought that's what agents were for, and I was wrong not to have more input. I was getting offers from other regional theaters, all of which were being handled by her. I stayed out of those negotiations, only to discover that she wasn't even negotiating—she was keeping them all at arm's length. Eventually, I found out why: she called me to say that there was a commercial producer who wanted to do the show Off-Broadway. That sounded fine to me, but only because I didn't realize all the repercussions of such an agreement. Not until I received the Option Agreement in the mail.

Options

What is an option? An option is the leasing of the rights to produce your play, until it is actually produced. You agree—in exchange for a negotiated payment—to give a theater or a producer the *exclusive* right to produce your play within an agreed length of time. !

As I mentioned previously, the word "exclusive" is an important one, because most options for premiere and/or New York productions have clauses that actively *prevent* other theatre companies from doing the work until the option expires. And that often takes between six and eighteen months. Time enough for those other interested parties to become much *less* interested.

There is also a typical clause in theatrical contracts that prevents the play from being produced by anyone else in the same geographical *region*. It doesn't even have to be a premiere! Strangely, this is an accepted practice that literally *prevents* playwrights from having their plays produced, except under severe limitations. As though it isn't hard enough already!

Do you see the problem? I was being presented with an offer by people I had never heard of, to essentially take my play *off the market*. Theatrical options still baffle me to this day.

I asked my agent about the terms of my option—these producers had a full year to produce my play, with no possibility of being done elsewhere as long as the option held. And even at the end of that year, there was no guarantee they would actually produce it; they could simply return the rights to me, and send me on my way. I asked her why she thought I should reject solid offers from numerous regional theatre companies, in the vague hope of being produced in New York. She said I answered my own question—"Because it's New York!" She was a New York agent in the old school sense. To her, productions didn't *matter* unless they happened in New York.

So I listened, and I signed the option agreement. My first mistake—and it was a big one. Options may sound good on paper, but never forget that the person who offers you an option is effectively *putting your play on hold*, while they scramble to get it together. A New York production might be your own ultimate goal, but it may also be an unwise step for an untested play. How will you know? Sorry, I don't have better advice than the following: you have to trust your gut. I can tell you this much—don't accept any offer on first impulse. Give yourself some time to think about it, and be sure to consider the possible repercussions.

Just before their option expired, nearly a year after I signed it, the producers agreed to exercise their rights to produce the play. How many productions had I kept at bay in the meantime? At least a half dozen—that I *knew* of.

Finding a Director

I suggested Bob Falls as the director, since he had shown such expertise and success with the play north of Chicago. But the producers never heard of him—that certainly wouldn't be the case today!—and they didn't have the money to put an out-of-towner in a hotel. (They had no money for me either; I was sleeping on the floor of a friend's apartment.) So they hired a New York director, one with good credits who seemed to like my script. I agreed to go along with their plan—and that was my second mistake.

Prior to rehearsal, meet with the director to make sure you're on the same page in regard to script work, as well as designs and casting. Make sure you see the play in similar ways. Establish what the rehearsal protocol will be, and ask his or her preferences about your method of communication during rehearsals. It's better to iron out any confusions or disagreements at this early stage, instead of waiting until actors are present.

Don't rely on hindsight—that's too late. And don't assume everyone knows better than you. As the history of performing arts has shown time and time again, they *don't*. Screenwriter William Goldman's famous statement about the movie business applies equally to theatre: "Nobody knows anything."[1]

The Performing Space

The producers paid for my plane ticket to New York, and I met the team, who all seemed very nice. Then I was escorted to the venue where the play would be produced—the Provincetown Playhouse in Greenwich Village. This was a historic Off-Broadway theater—the place where O'Neill did some of his earliest plays,

---

[1]William Goldman. *Adventures in the Screen Trade: A Personal View of Hollywood and Screenwriting.* New York: Warner, 1983. Print.

and where Edward Albee's *The Zoo Story* premiered on a double bill with Samuel Beckett's *Krapp's Last Tape*. But it had seen better days. By now it was rundown, with uncomfortable seating and an ancient heating system, which sounded like a 737 taking off whenever the furnace kicked into gear. And the show was being produced in a very cold November, so that noise would be blasting throughout our run. There was no money in the production budget to remodel the theater, as was sorely needed.

They asked me what I thought, which was a kind gesture. So I agreed to the venue—my third mistake.

Theater spaces make a difference. This is one area in which you will almost never have a say, and probably shouldn't expect to. After all, you're thrilled to have your show produced at all—what matter does it make where it's performed?

It matters. Again, not that you'll be in a position to do anything about it, but an unwelcoming or uncomfortable theater space will negatively affect your play. I've had plays performed in what were essentially concrete bunkers, with acoustics so poor that the actors' voices bounced off the walls with unstoppable echoes. I've also had plays in theaters where there were other plays in the next theater, or even worse, parties.

And yes, size matters too. Given the choice between a large theater and a smaller one, playwrights will nearly always pick the larger one. There's more potential to make money there, since writers usually receive royalties (more on that later). But that may not always be the best choice. Believe me, you'd rather have your play sell out in a 200-seat theater than sell 200 seats in a 800-seat theater. Same amount of audience, but one feels like a hit, and the other looks like a bomb. In addition, a four-character play may perform like gangbusters in the smaller theater, but be lost in the cavernous space of the larger one.

In short, try not to jump at a production when it's offered to you—examine the details and consider the potential consequences! !

Casting

After we checked out the Provincetown Playhouse, we moved across town to the auditions, which surprisingly turned out to be for only two of the three roles. When I asked why we weren't auditioning for the lead role, the producers looked at each other with some embarrassment. It was then that I learned—for the first time—that one of the producers intended to play the main role *himself*. Indeed, that was the reason my play was optioned in the first place! Even the director was flabbergasted that no one had told me; as the playwright, I was supposed to have approval over casting. But no one had told me about this.

I called my agent, who shrugged it off. "What do you want me to do? Call it off?" Clearly, she had known this was the plan all along. Whether she forgot to mention it, or whether it was an intentional omission, I never discovered. The man who wanted the role tried to assure me by declaring he would be a "silent" producer—not listed in the program or any of the publicity—so no one would know of his involvement and label our production as a "vanity" project. This didn't give me much confidence, but everyone was telling me to go along with it. I didn't have one ally who encouraged me to question this unusual plan. So once again, thinking everyone must know better than me, I reluctantly gave my consent. That was my fourth mistake.

Do Playwrights Have Any Say?

This seems like a good time to discuss casting, approval of artistic staff, and other aspects involving a playwright's participation in a production. I will begin by alluding to ment—the playwright's "Bill of Rights," as

A.[2] All beginning playwrights should read it

eed does a very effective job of addressing

new playwrights, about the "business"

ction.

es that the playwright is the sole legal

no changes to the text are allowed

ion from the author. In addition, it is

wright has open access to casting and

his document gives playwrights much

might imagine even possessing—*in*

theo

The D   's important to remember. However,
the Gu   ablished because of the rampant
exploita   s. Screenwriters do have a union,
which p   **New**   y writing job for film or television.
Playwrigh   ame kind of legal protection. But
what play wrights do have, as opposed to other kinds of dramatic
writers, is *ownership*. As it clearly states in the "Bill of Rights,"
playwrights *own* their plays. If you're under the impression a TV
or film writer owns their scripts, think again. Wait until the final
credits roll, and one of the last things you'll read is the copyright,
which is usually assigned to the studio or production company.
So in place of the substantial income that can be made in TV or
film, playwrights are awarded the actual ownership of their own
dramatic writing. No one can mess with it, or claim authorship,
or steal it. Huzzah!

But wait. As I just mentioned, the Guild isn't a union. So playwrights
sometimes have difficulty enforcing their rights. These rules
aren't laws; they're highly recommended suggestions. If theaters
choose to defy the playwright or disregard his or her wishes, the

---

[2]"Dramatists Guild | Bill of Rights." *Dramatists Guild | Bill of Rights.* N.p., n.d. Web.
November 10, 2014.

only practical right a playwright usually has is to pull the show and shut down the production.

Fortunately, most theaters respect and honor the guidelines of the DGA, and it's generally understood that they are expected to follow the basic Guild contracts. But not always.

In 2014, there was an astounding controversy involving *Hands on a Hardbody*, a new musical which had a Broadway run. The artistic director of a theater in Texas produced the show, but decided himself that the songs needed to be in a whole new order. The creators of the show (Amanda Green, Trey Anastasio, and Doug Wright) understandably protested, and the production was shut down. I wish I could say this is an outrageously unusual example of exploiting dramatic writers, but it's not. I myself have had two shows open and run—in major regional theaters—without those theatres first acquiring permission and paying for the performance rights . . . two that I *know* of.

Back to my own production in New York. Did I have the right to stop things in their tracks? Absolutely. But I weighed it against time already invested and expenses already paid—including option money and an advance against the box office that had already been paid to me. In all truth, I was living hand to mouth, and much of that money was already spent and gone on such extravagant luxuries as rent and utilities on my unfurnished apartment back in Minneapolis. I was also unduly influenced by the fact that the producers all seemed to like the play—something that means so much when you're young and vulnerable. I decided not to throw a wrench into the works, and have faith that it would all work out.

It didn't. And as I said, my fourth mistake.

Bad Rehearsals

Rehearsals in New York were tense. Nobody seemed very happy, and there seemed to be a lack of trust between the director and the actors, as well as the director and the playwright. Early on I was admonished by the director not to interfere with his process, and to hold any thoughts or suggestions until the Equity break. He even asked me to move when I sat behind him in the theater; he wanted me to sit several rows away. This was a very different experience from the one I had with Robert Falls, and I couldn't understand why.

Again, my relative lack of experience compelled me to obey. I complied with the director's wishes, and obeyed his personal version of rehearsal protocol. When the director suggested we add a song to the play toward the end—a maudlin version of "Amazing Grace," for some reason—I was dumbfounded and didn't understand the purpose. But I thought he must know better. Today, of course, with much more experience under my belt, I would probably pull the show altogether or discuss the dismissal of the director with the producers (admittedly harder to do when one of them is also your lead actor!). I shut up, and for the most part sat quietly in the back of the theater. That was my fifth mistake.

Let's be clear about this.

You have the right to be at rehearsal.   !

You have the right to express your suggestions and opinions to the director, and to the cast, as long as you don't cause interruptions, disruptions, or discord.

You have the right to reject suggestions and opinions proffered to you (though you should be wise enough to consider all input with openness and flexibility).

You have the right to make changes late in the rehearsal process (in consultation with the director and the acting company).

Most importantly, you have the right to enjoy the rehearsal process, and to learn from it.

Sometime during technical rehearsals, when I was quietly sitting in the dark and wishing I was somewhere else, the board operator brought me a handwritten note. He told me it was from "some guy" who had come in and watched a few minutes of rehearsal from the back of the house. Reading the note, I discovered that Bob Falls himself had come in and watched for a while. He didn't want to "disturb" anyone, and left without saying a word.

I was ashamed of myself. Bob was the man who should have been directing my play, with the Chicago cast that performed so brilliantly at Wisdom Bridge. What was my play doing here with these strangers? Then I began to think about how Falls himself might have felt, and whether he felt betrayed and pushed aside. His note was friendly, and he wished me and the play good fortune, but my sense of shame only grew. Why hadn't I insisted that he be the director? Or better yet, why didn't I give him a chance to direct it at one of the regional theaters that had been lobbying to produce it?

I mention this only to emphasize the following point:

Relationships with other artists are crucially important to any playwright—so do your best to maintain them when those people display a special understanding of you and your writing. Be careful about making decisions that discard those people, even when it appears to be professionally expedient. Trust your gut when you're asked to choose. Loyalty is crucial in the theatre, and almost always should be maintained!

Similarly, be smart and don't hesitate to move on from people who don't share your artistic vision, or that you feel are holding you back in any way. That could include directors, producers, or agents. Again, if something feels wrong . . . it probably is! And such situations can arise without warning, when you least expect it. Be prepared.

As I've described, it became clearer and clearer to me that I was in a debilitating position during rehearsals in New York. I felt horrible and embarrassed by my own inexperience and stupidity. I should have *known* better.

And I was getting angry—especially at myself. Not helpful, believe me. It's easier said than done, but try not to get mad, or at least don't let others see you get mad. Losing your cool *never* works in the theatre. And I've seen it happen a hundred times. It makes everyone uncomfortable, causes doubt in the minds of the artists, and makes work that is already underpaid and highly stressful even harder to endure. There's a theatrical cliché that acrimonious productions tend to be more successful—don't you believe it.

By all means, you have every right to express your convictions forcefully, even passionately. But if you need to release anger, take a long walk away from the theater. Otherwise you'll be faced with another cliché—and this one is quite accurate—about burning bridges. You can light that match before you even realize it. !

The show began previews. We "papered" the house (offered free tickets) on Halloween night, and a surreal crowd of homeless patrons from the Bowery, cross-dressers, witches, and punk rockers showed up to watch the show. The show in the audience was more fascinating than the one on stage. One man kept his gorilla suit—including the head—on for the whole performance. Not easy to do, since the gas furnace made it feel about 85 degrees in the theater.

Because the lobby of the Provincetown Playhouse was so tiny, and the weather outside was frigid, the director decided to remove the intermission and make the play a straight run of 100 minutes. That may sound short, but it felt very long in that boiling heat—especially with the addition of the "song."

On opening night, I sat right behind the *New York Post* drama critic Clive Barnes, who apparently was overcome by the constant white noise of the blower and the oppressiveness of the heat. He promptly fell asleep after five minutes, and woke up about five minutes from the end. I had a terrible premonition, and for good reason. The opening night party had a grim feel, and we all stayed long enough to get the late edition of the *New York Times*. No review. The director seemed relieved: "No news is good news."

The following day, my family arrived, my parents excited about their son's New York debut, and with heightened expectations that the show would be an unqualified hit. They saw the next performance after opening night, and their reaction afterwards was a bit muted. "Seemed like it went a little better in Chicago," my dad said in his understated but totally candid way.

Then we went out to celebrate at a restaurant in Little Italy. I couldn't concentrate on the meal; I kept thinking about that damned *Times* review, and whether it would be in the late edition of the *Times*. As soon as the main course was over, and people had ordered dessert, I rushed outside and bought the paper from a newsstand. I stood there and read it. My—how many by now?—*sixth* mistake.

My worst fears were confirmed. The review (by Mel Gussow) was buried at the bottom of the inside of the Arts section. It was three short paragraphs, completely dismissive. The most complimentary remark was when Gussow expressed appreciation for my courage in giving it a title that contained the word "losing." Which he felt was an appropriate description for the show.

What About Critics?

I actually have a nice story about critics. Once upon a time, I had a show in a small theater that couldn't afford much publicity.

On the night of the final preview, there was a blizzard. The house was empty at curtain time. So the director and the artistic staff were just about to cancel the show altogether, when in walked three newspaper critics! Well, that was that; the actors performed the show for three critics, one nervous director, and one terrified playwright. And those three critics couldn't have been nicer to me, talking to me before the show and at intermission, recognizing the humor of the situation. Even their subsequent reviews were kind and appreciative, taking into consideration the absurdity of it all. That's when I learned some critics are actually kind and sympathetic human beings, and won't kick a person when he's down. I was lucky.

But I haven't always been that lucky, and you shouldn't expect to be either. As much as is humanly possible, DON'T READ REVIEWS. Having said that, all caps or not, you will inevitably read them. I can't stop you. DON'T DO IT. But you will.

Since you will read them (but DON'T!), try to put them in perspective. Theatre critics (an endangered species, to be sure), are trying to provide a service to their readers, as well as to the arts organizations that continue to give them a reason to be employed. That's a conflict of interest right there. And that's the reason the majority of reviews are neither raves nor pans, but are mostly what are called "mixed" reviews: the "I liked it, but . . ." response. It makes them appear to be thoughtful and professional. So you should usually expect to receive that type of review.

The best and most meaningful reviews are ones that openly acknowledge the audience response. Why? Because the audience is there without an agenda—they paid real money, they want to enjoy it, and they don't want to feel they wasted their time.

Some critics, unfortunately, resent the audience reaction. They prefer to set themselves above or apart from the audience, and insist on their analytical superiority to the unwashed masses. A play that results in thunderous applause and standing ovations might be depicted as pandering to the audience. Conversely, a play that results in massive walkouts and tepid (or even angry) responses is sometimes described as a brilliant work that challenges and enlightens the unwilling crowd. This critic isn't just reviewing the show. This critic is reviewing the *audience*, in the most condescending fashion imaginable. Again, my favorite critics don't ignore *or* assess the audience; they *reflect* them.

This dichotomy happens all the time. Like most playwrights, I've had a few productions that were embraced by their audiences, of which I was enormously proud, that got trashed by the press. But the opposite also occurs, and is much worse, in my opinion. Occasionally, I'm invited to visit revivals of my plays, and these are sometimes uncomfortable experiences. I can tell that the show isn't good within a few minutes. It's clear that the audience is politely tolerating it at best, or hostile at worst. So I'm disturbed if the critics decide to give it an unqualified rave. This tells me that those critics don't pay the slightest attention to what's happening around them. I suppose I should feel lucky to escape castigation, but I feel like a fraud whenever that happens.

As the playwright, you cannot afford to be affected by reviews. !

They can certainly affect the box office, which will affect the financial success of your show. But otherwise, they have nothing to do with you. It's an old aphorism, but one that still rings true: if you believe your good reviews, you'll have to believe the bad ones too. So don't do it. Don't read them (DON'T!), but if you do (and you will) don't believe them. Chances are—at least after years of experience—you'll know *yourself* how well the show is working, and you won't need input to figure it out.

The audience is the key. Don't ignore them, or set out to alienate them. Respect them. Learn to listen to the !

audience as you rewrite and rework the show. And you'll make it better.

How Do You Deal With Failure?

Good question. Which brings me back to that newsstand in Little Italy. Reading my own review—especially at such an inopportune moment—was my final mistake. I came back to the restaurant and proceeded to ruin everyone's mood. My family tried unsuccessfully to get me to ignore the review and enjoy our limited time together, but that was my first taste of critical rejection, and it hit me hard.

After a few weeks of struggling to promote the show by using some nice reviews from other papers, the producers threw in the towel and ended the run. Regional theaters sent the scripts back within a week or two—even the ones who had already asked for the rights!—suddenly indicating they "couldn't find room" for the play in their season schedules. The movie studios and TV producers followed suit—they decided to "move on."

A friend of mine, living in Manhattan, noticed the big wooden marquee sign for *Losing It* sticking out of a dumpster next to the Provincetown Playhouse. He was actually kind enough to rescue it and carry it to his apartment building until he could call me to see whether I wanted it. I didn't. So my play literally went into the dumpster.

But wait. It did get one more production that same year—at a very prestigious regional theater in Texas. And guess what? They "forgot" to secure the rights, and I knew nothing about it until a writer in residence at the Playwrights' Center told me he had seen it advertised. To add insult to injury, they had cut the script to an hour, so it could be featured as lunchtime theatre for the downtown office workers. Cutting it without permission may have had something to do with "forgetting" to get the rights, don't you think? This is why there's a DGA.

Here was my compromise when I called the theater: I allowed them to continue to perform the shortened version, but I wanted to be paid for it. Against my better judgment (and my previous advice to you), I went to the library (no internet yet!) and allowed myself to read the reviews from Texas. Believe it or not, they were raves. Did it work better as a one-act play? Possibly. I'll never know. I didn't go see it, nor was I invited.

The failure of a first play would have been the end of many writers' careers. But I was determined to bounce back, somehow, someday. Why? Call it hubris, call it determination, call it stupidity. But eventually, I had another hit on my hands—this time with much less stressful results. The important thing is, I licked my wounds and tried again.

"Success"

"Success" (still a word that's hard for me to use without quotation marks) is uncontrollable, unpredictable, and to a large extent—when it happens—unavoidable. But a beginning playwright would be well advised to understand the following principles:

a You will find "success"—or happiness, or fulfillment, or accomplishment—easier to achieve if you don't rely on other's definitions of what it entails.

b It's not about having "buzz."

c It's not about getting your name in the paper.

d It's not about awards or nominations.

e It's not about ticket sales or royalty checks.

f It's not even about productions—either in number or quality.

It is about *the writing itself*—no more, and no less. A writer who has finished a work and is excited by its progress, has found *true meaning* in his or her work—that's the only definition of success that I recognize, for myself or others.

Other people will, of course, have their own definitions, and they will try to impose those definitions on you and your work. Don't insult them by telling them this, but their opinions *just don't matter*. They may affect publicity, your chances for production, or even your box office—but they cannot and should not affect *you*.

How do you deal with failure? The same way the Chicago Cubs did for so long until they actually won the World Series again—*perseverance*. Realize that all setbacks are temporary. And move on, with renewed determination. Get back on the damn horse. I'm proud to say I got back on mine.

Points to Remember

- Be careful about option agreements, and be able to negotiate the terms (especially length of the option).
- Be aware of how different theater spaces can affect the production.
- Be sure to begin your relationship with the director *before* rehearsals begin, to make sure you're on the same page.
- Learn your rights as a playwright, especially those outlined by the DGA. Speak up if they're being ignored or thwarted.
- Don't let your relative inexperience make you hesitant to question any part of the theatrical process which gives you doubts. All playwrights must be vigilant against exploitation. So if you feel something isn't right—in a contract, in casting, in rehearsal—then you have the right to question the situation. Artistic compromise may

sometimes be required, but it's up to you to weigh the potential results, and the balance of what you gain in exchange for what you sacrifice. Give yourself some time to think about it, and be sure to consider the possible repercussions.

- Successful personal relationships are crucial in the theatre. If one turns sour, try to repair it to whatever extent you can, but don't try to save it at the expense of your play. Most of all, there's no justification for losing one's temper, no matter who's in the right. Its destructive effects are unavoidable, especially if done in front of an acting company.

- Don't read reviews. DON'T! But if you do, remember that they usually have little to do with you and your writing process. Remember that the good ones are just as irrelevant as the bad ones; treat them with equal disinterest. Audience response is all that matters.

- Failure is a state of mind, and dependent on your personal definition of "success." Don't let anyone else define it for you.

7 Publishing and Professional Decisions

Publishing

Many people ask—when is a playwright done with a play? I heard one famous playwright answer that question this way: "I'm never done with a play. But eventually the play is done with me."

A more answer is whenever he or she gets the play published. In America, the publishing company leases the rights to produce the play, and the published script is usually considered to be the final production draft. Most plays that manage to get more than one or two productions have a good chance of being published by one of the major firms: Samuel French, Dramatists Play Service, Playscripts, or Broadway Play Publishing. After their scripts get published, playwrights usually let go of their plays, and don't necessarily participate in subsequent productions (except by invitation).

How Do You Protect Your Writing?

In these days of posting scripts online, it becomes even more important to protect the ownership of your work. Play thefts aren't as pervasive as scripts for film and television, where there are regular court cases claiming appropriation of "intellectual properties," but it still behooves any dramatist to prevent someone from stealing or using their play without permission.

Certainly, before you send a script to *anyone*—even a best friend or family member—you should protect yourself against accidental or intentional theft.

The two best ways of legally protecting one's work in the United States haven't changed in decades: US Copyright registration, or script registration with the Writers Guild of America (WGA) (West or East). Both are inexpensive and available online.[1]

Most people will recommend applying for a copyright through the Library of Congress—it's a one-time permanent registration, good for the entire life of the copyright (the playwright's lifetime plus seventy years). The other advantage happens in the unlikely event that you enter into a lawsuit claiming copyright infringement. If your work is copyrighted, you can claim additional damages above and beyond the actual money that should have come to you instead of the thief.

A few disadvantages of a copyright, compared with registration at the WGA, is that it costs a bit more to apply, it takes several months to receive confirmation (though you are protected as of the day the Copyright Office receives your materials), and if there are any changes in your script at any time, you have to *replace* your old copyright with a new one. This can be a bit annoying to a publisher if you inform them that your play is already copyrighted, and they have to go through the replacement process when copyrighting the *book version* of your play. In addition, it's a lengthier and more difficult process to get access to your materials, once deposited at the Library of Congress.

The WGA, by comparison, is a streamlined process that gives you instant confirmation. They accept stage plays for registration, as well as other forms of dramatic writing. Once you register with them, they keep it on file for five years before destroying it and

---

[1] http://www.wgawregistry.org/; https://www.wgaeast.org/script_registration; http://www.copyright.gov/register/performing.html

removing it from their files. The biggest disadvantage is that you will need to *remember* to renew your registration before it expires—and they will not send you a reminder. For that reason, I like to use WGA registration as a way of protecting my works in progress. You can keep submitting subsequent drafts at any interval, and they will all receive the same level of protection.

It's also easier to gain access to your materials at any point during the registration period (which you may need if your computer crashes, for example). And being registered there makes it an easier process for a publisher to copyright your work once you get a book deal. Finally, you don't have to be a member of the Guild (that won't be necessary for your play until someone decides to turn it into a film or television show— at which point your Guild membership will be deducted from your first payment).

No need to do both a copyright and a WGA registration, of course. Just make sure you do it one way or the other, before sending your scripts out into the world!

What About Contracts?

Since most beginning writers don't have agents to negotiate for them, they can freak out when they get a look at their first production contract. It's often several pages long, even for small non-Equity productions. Basically, the theater promises—in writing—to produce your play for a set number of performances at a given time. In exchange for the rights to produce your work, they will pay you a fee.

For small non-Equity companies, that may be a very small fee indeed. This is where you'll have to decide if it's personally worth it to you. If a theater offers you fifty dollars (or free tickets in lieu of any monetary payment), you may feel insulted. On the other hand, if you're anxious to have your play seen by audiences and reviewed, possibly leading to other productions, then the minimal payment may be offset by your willingness to have the experience. Many non-professional theaters will offer you a certain fee per show—say, $25 a performance. That's usually a better deal for you, but keep in mind they prefer to do that in case the play doesn't sell and they have to *cancel* performances. You won't get any money for cancelled shows.

If it's at a professional regional theater, you will probably receive a version of the standard DGA contract. This contract will break down your royalty percentage, usually based on the number of actual tickets sold, with a minimum guarantee. So obviously, a large theater with a long run is going to make you more money. But sometimes playwrights turn down a bigger theater for the chance to work with someone they know at a smaller venue. And as I mentioned before, sometimes a smaller theater space is preferable for a better audience experience. Don't always assume bigger is better.

In any case, big or small, professional or non-professional, a production contract should always include a few standard provisions protecting your rights as a playwright. Again, these are offered by the standard DGA contract, and they have a version for amateur and non-professional productions you can access online (as long as you're a member of the DGA, of course).

These rights include:

- The right to have your name listed on all advertising.
- The right to preserve your text as written, unless you give explicit permission or suggest the changes yourself. This insures that no one can change the text in your absence, or even after the show opens.
- The right to attend rehearsals. Whether or not they pay you a per diem to allow you to be at rehearsal, you have

a right to attend, even if it means you pay your own expenses (and it might).

- The right to be consulted on a director, and then to be consulted on casting. Obviously, if you don't live in the same town as the production, this will be more difficult to accomplish. But you can still ask to be informed and kept in the loop.

- And possibly the right to a number of free tickets for the opening and during the run. That number can be negotiated, based on your needs.

Also, watch out for "red flags" in contracts. A typical offender comes under the category of subsidiary rights, which allows a theater to take a percentage of the writer's proceeds for a certain period of time. This still tends to be a fairly common practice, for theaters to receive a piece of the action if they do the show first. That's not usually a lot of money—unless the play becomes a big hit. Joseph Papp's cut of two shows that began at the Public Theater—*Hair* and *A Chorus Line*—financed his theater for many years. And for many years afterwards, that made every other theater in the country want to jump on the bandwagon. As you might imagine, this has become a highly controversial subject, since many contemporary playwrights have questioned the justification for taking a slice out of the writer's income. As a result, a growing number of major theaters have decided to eschew all participation in future royalties, including Lincoln Center Theater in New York City, Center Theatre Group in Los Angeles, and Steppenwolf Theater in Chicago.

For a small theater to ask for *any* subsidiary rights is a pretty outrageous demand, but some of them have been known to ask for one to five years of future participation, or even longer. No beginning playwright should ever cave in to such greed— the DGA would suggest passing on such a production, and so would I. If they want to do your play badly enough, they won't insist.

Also, be careful if they want to extend their exclusive option on your play beyond the closing date of the production. Some theaters insert such a clause in case your play becomes a hit, and they would either like to extend the run or move the production to another venue. Those are both wonderful scenarios, and it's good that the theater is thinking positively—but I can't imagine any reason for allowing a theater to prevent other productions for longer than three months (*maybe* six if they're a powerhouse). A Broadway production, of course, is quite different—a commercial run with the potential to run for years (if you're very, very lucky).

The notion that a playwright may be faced with unavoidable choices that will determine the future path of his or her writing comes as a shock to many beginning writers.

It's crucial to be prepared. Seek advice, be informed, but remember in the end, you will have to live with your own decisions. Gut instinct should not be undervalued. If good things happen, you should be smart about what to do about it—and it's easier than you might think to be unprepared.

Does Geography Matter?

I spent the better part of my artistic life traveling from American city to city, going wherever there seemed to be interest in my work. People are dumbfounded when I tell them about my residential itinerary, all determined by schooling, productions, grants, and teaching gigs: Louisville, Nashville, Manhattan, Long Island, Bloomington (Indiana), back to Louisville, St. Louis, back to Manhattan, Minneapolis, Chicago, Atlanta, Seattle, Austin, back to Seattle, back to Manhattan *again*, Los Angeles, and Washington, DC. Does my life sound a bit peripatetic? Do I recommend that kind of lifestyle for a developing writer? In retrospect, no.

An itinerant lifestyle—ready to drive, fly, or hitchhike to any town doing your work—may be an understandable temptation. It was for me. After all, if nothing seems to be happening for you wherever you're at, why not go someplace else where your writing is getting more attention? It's a good theory, but based on my experience, much too disruptive. Every time I moved, I thought I had found the answer to what I was searching for. But in the long run, it probably wasn't worth the personal sacrifices I had to make. Moving every few years wreaks havoc on personal relationships, finances, and one's sense of stability. If the idea of community is important to you, then don't feel the need to upend it. You can literally be a writer anywhere, and you can choose where you want to live; don't let others influence you unless you're truly ready to move on.

The late August Wilson surprised a lot of people after he achieved success on Broadway. Many theatre folks assumed he would be moving from Minnesota to New York City. But he went the opposite direction, to Seattle. I understood why, having once lived there myself for seven years. It's a beautiful city, conducive to writing (usually overcast, which encourages you to stay home and churn out pages, with occasional sojourns to coffee shops and bookstores). And he had an informal, ongoing commitment to produce his work at Seattle Rep—sometimes *before* the plays went to Broadway. It's important for every writer to find the place that feels like home, and Seattle became August's home until his untimely death.

On the other hand, many playwrights begin in one-horse towns from which they can't wait to escape. I've met many of them in each and every city I've lived in. But there's only one place where proximity has historically given playwrights a definite advantage, and that's New York City. For film and television, of course, it's Los Angeles. But here's the thing I'd like to suggest—if you're happy wherever you are, and you feel there's sufficient interest in your work (either locally or elsewhere) to sustain you, then stay put. Be happy with who you are, and what you've got. Changing your place of residence is not necessarily the solution to advancing your life as a playwright.

Speaking of which . . .

Can a Playwright Make Bad Decisions?

Earlier in this book I mentioned the unfortunate phenomenon of "premieritis," which actually prevented subsequent productions of popular plays. I ran into this problem a few times in my career. *T Bone N Weasel* received simultaneous offers from ATL and Manhattan Theatre Club; and *Dimly Perceived Threats to the System* received simultaneous interest from three theaters in Washington, DC, as well as American Repertory Theater in Cambridge. It didn't matter that both plays had already received their first productions in Minneapolis; those were considered to be "non-professional," since they both operated under contracts that allowed Equity actors to appear as "guests," so the subsequent theaters were battling over rights to the first "Professional Premiere." As I said before, the importance of such wording can become strangely significant, at least to the producing theaters.

In the end, I chose ATL's Humana Festival for the first play, and Arena Stage for the second. I have no regrets about those choices, but I was disappointed that I had to sacrifice four other productions in the process. A few years after the premiere of *T Bone N Weasel*, after scores of successful regional productions, I called Manhattan Theatre Club and asked if they'd still be interested in the New York premiere. No sale. Since then, the play has had somewhere in the vicinity of a hundred productions around the country—but to date, none in Manhattan.

So the question arises: Did I make the right decision regarding my play? Should I have taken the risk of allowing my play to be produced in New York first? If successful there, my "career" trajectory might have launched into jet drive. My name might have become better known, and I might have received more commissions and offers to write for film and television (emphasizing the uncertainty of the word "might").

On the other hand—and this is something Jon Jory convinced me of—I'd be taking the risk of putting my play into instant jeopardy, since one bad review from the *New York Times* could erase its future overnight. After my experience with *Losing It* (in addition to my personal attachment to ATL), Jory didn't have to persuade me for long. And as I said, I've continued to have productions of *T Bone N Weasel* to this day. So I don't harbor many regrets, just occasional curious speculation.

Now allow me to tell you about the worst decision I ever made—one that will probably make you conclude that I'm a madman, and prompt you to throw this book across the room. As far as I know, I may be the only playwright in history to *turn down* the Eugene O'Neill National Playwrights Conference.

If I haven't made clear already, the O'Neill Conference is probably the most important play development program in the country. Many important playwrights have got their professional start by having their first plays showcased there. So I should have been thrilled, back in the late 1990s, when my play *Dimly Perceived Threats to the System* was picked to be showcased there.

Instead, the timing made me hesitate, since it conflicted a bit with my premiere production of *Octopus* at the Contemporary American Theater Festival in West Virginia. This was a play based on a true story, a current event which had received national attention, about the mysterious death of a freelance investigative journalist. Due to my personal relationship with the reporters who broke the story, I had acquired the rights to dramatize the events. So I wrote a stage play, landed a production, and was hopeful that this would be just the first step in a long series of productions around the country, including New York.

I was very invested in *Octopus*—probably *too* invested. When I got the call from the O'Neill Conference that *Dimly Perceived Threats* had been selected, my initial delight was dampened when I heard the rehearsal schedule. There would be a one-week overlap with my rehearsals for *Octopus*. Was I required to be present at the O'Neill for the entire time? Yes, she said. Were there no exceptions, under no circumstances? Even a conflicting production? "You'll have to decide," she replied, "between the O'Neill and your production. It will have to be okay for you to miss a week of rehearsal for your other show. We can't make an exception." So in the pressure to make a fast decision, I made the wrong one. I passed.

Don't feel too sorry for me; *Dimly Perceived Threats* went on to several other productions. However, I watched as new crops of playwrights broke through to national exposure for the next several years, the result of their participation at the O'Neill Conference. As time went on, it was clear that I had been shortsighted.

Like many things in life, what feels tremendously significant and crucial in the moment often loses its importance over time. A very hard skill to develop is awareness of what will become or remain important to you over time. Don't sacrifice valuable opportunities because of difficult timing or inconvenience. Try to imagine what will be more meaningful to you in five years, or ten.

Guess what? That wasn't my only bad decision. I've also turned down a Broadway production. (Steven Dietz once told me I have a habit of rejecting opportunities most other writers would kill for, which seems to indicate a serious lack of intelligence on my part.)

Southern Cross is an epic play about a gigantic subject. Covering 150 years of Southern history, it takes a look at the river of time as events stream back and forth from the Civil War to the Civil Rights era. Several historical figures are featured in parallel stories that intersect in echoes of time: Huey Long, Martin Luther King, General Tecumseh Sherman, and Elvis Presley. A few common themes persist throughout the play: those of exploitation, injustice, and violence.

The idea came about when I felt like writing something huge, so I did so. Probably the most ridiculously impractical play I've ever written, with over forty characters (extensive doubling obviously required). After the premiere production at Illusion Theater in Minneapolis, I was lucky enough to receive an individual award from the National Endowment for the Arts (when such awards were possible; individual awards were discontinued shortly thereafter). After the production at Alliance Theater in Atlanta, *Southern Cross* also made the Ten Best List in *Time* magazine.

As a result of the *Time* magazine mention, I got a call from Gerald Schoenfeld. He was the chairman of the Shubert Organization, which owned seventeen Broadway theaters at the time of his death in 2008. He told me that he was interested in producing it on Broadway . . . if I would turn it into a musical.

I was taken aback. The play had already been published in an acting edition, it had won awards and a citation by *Time* magazine, so I was reluctant to mess with it. I also had a snobbish attitude toward musicals, thinking that they were generally manipulative and sentimental. I couldn't imagine my precious play being marred with actual songs (even if Elvis Presley was a character!).

So I politely passed. I remember him saying, "I don't want to make you do anything that doesn't feel right to you." Which was exactly the right thing for him to say, and should have been the thing to make me stop in my tracks and say, "Wait a minute. Let's talk about this." But no, my arrogance and narrow-mindedness prevented me from making an intelligent decision. I spoke out of misguided pride, and I gave up a once-in-a-lifetime opportunity.

Shortly thereafter, one of my favorite novels, E. L. Doctorow's *Ragtime*, became a very successful musical on Broadway, and I began to realize the extent of my error. Musical theatre has a power and attraction that often can't be matched by straight plays. I know that now—but I didn't know it then. Who was I to be so arrogant?

When faced with a professional decision, try to leave your ego out of it. Such an offer or opportunity may catch you at a time of personal crisis, or at a point of enormous success. Pay no attention to either. Your decisions need to be free of emotional clutter, with an eye on the future. Think about the long-term consequences (admittedly easier said than done!).

How Do You Earn a Living?

Having already brought up the crass subject of income, I should probably talk about playwriting and financial survival. But those subjects seem contradictory. How can you do both at once?

Obviously, any way you can. Still, I would encourage you to find a job that leaves you creative energy in your off hours. In this respect, being a playwright is easier than being an actor. Actors have to be free during the day for auditions and rehearsals, and as a result they often have temporary employment. Playwrights, like any other writer, can write in their own time—though I do recommend trying to work out a flexible arrangement so that you can be available for rehearsals, if you're fortunate enough to land a production.

I worked in box offices, bookstores, and as a temp worker for a bank, a media company, and a hospital. The temp agencies were usually very good about understanding if I had to leave on short notice, but they didn't provide any health benefits for that very reason.

After some stage production experience, I found part-time work teaching at writers' centers and extension programs at universities. None of that made me rich, but it did give me more time to work on my own writing. As a matter of fact, doing part-time work made me more productive, since I was aware of how my own time was restricted.

You will find that your own writing schedules are based largely on what little time you have free from your jobs and family commitments. That's as it should be; use your own time wisely.

Time Management

Here's what I learned as a fledgling playwright, which I now pass on to you.

Do whatever it takes to survive—while making sure you have the means to write.

That means:

a Finding a place to live that you can afford, and that may mean living with roommates, friends, family, lovers, or benefactors to help you share the costs, if necessary.

b Finding a job that won't drive you crazy with stress or exhaustion, and will let you create a regular, dependable writing schedule. Maybe your writing schedule will be squeezed in before work, maybe after work, maybe weekends only. You decide. But—this is important—*use your free time wisely*. Easier said than done, no doubt about it.

c   Staying focused, and not getting too distracted or forgetting your goals.

Basically, it means that with everything else going on in your life—including the demands of loved ones—you must protect and preserve your own time. Because your time is the Time You Will Write.

All this will be hard to maintain. You should expect that. But try your best!

Points to Remember

- You don't have to consider your play "finished" until after it's published—perhaps not even then!

- Be sure to protect your written material by registering your scripts, either with the US Copyright Office or the WGA.

- If you're fortunate enough to receive a production, peruse the contract carefully and run it by the eyes of an agent or a lawyer, to be sure you're being treated fairly in the long term. You should be aware of the rights secured in your behalf by the DGA—read their "Bill of Rights" to become familiar with them.

- You don't have to uproot yourself for a career as a playwright, though many have. Just remember it's entirely possible to pursue a life in the theatre without disrupting your personal life.

- When faced with important decisions and choices regarding production conflicts and offers, be sure to take a little time to consider them well. If someone wants you or your play that badly, they can wait a day or two.

- Do what it takes to survive—physically and financially— without sacrificing the time you need to write your plays.

- Time is valuable—learn not to waste it on pointless, stubborn notions of ideas that you are determined to make work, despite all evidence to the contrary. Listen to your gut—if it's telling you you're making a mistake, you probably are. Don't fritter away any more time on such a doubt-filled project—move on, and feel good about doing so!

8 Building a Reputation

How Do You Bounce Back?

First of all, in the wake of a flop, it takes mental discipline not to get angry or overwhelmed with feelings of injustice. And I'll admit that it's so much easier for me to say that in retrospect. At the time of my New York failure, and my humbled retreat back to Minnesota, I couldn't shake the predominance of two extreme emotions: either (a) I wanted to kill somebody (critics, producers, successful playwrights, New Yorkers, people who stared at me for no reason, etc.), or (b) I wanted to die. I had that timelessly horrible combination of rage and self-pity.

But it doesn't take long to get bored with emotional extremes. Soon I began to write again. Fortunately, I found Minneapolis a very forgiving place, and there was still interest in my new plays there. No one in the upper Midwest seemed to care what happened in my New York debut. How did I manage to drum up renewed enthusiasm to write? Like many other creative people, by making a conscious decision to view my "failure" as a learning experience.

Here are two familiar quotes about failure:

a "Our doubts are traitors, and make us lose the good we oft might win, by fearing to attempt."—William Shakespeare[1]

---

[1] From *Measure for Measure*.

b "Ever tried. Ever failed. No matter. Try Again. Fail again. Fail better."—Samuel Beckett[2]

Let's face it, the list of "failed" plays that went on to become enormously successful is remarkable. Initial works by Aristophanes, Shaw, Ibsen, Chekhov, O'Neill, Pinter, Hellman, even the first production of Sam Shepard's *True West* (his most frequently produced play) were all greeted with scorn and ridicule when first presented.

Financial Considerations

So let's outlaw such a meaningless word as "failure," subject to a thousand variations and interpretations (second only to "success"). There's only one aspect of failure that can be accurately attributed to a production, and that's the financial one. Either it makes money or it doesn't. That's clear enough. But we all know there are terrible plays that can make a lot of money (especially if they have television or film stars attached), and there are terrific plays that can't seem to attract a paying audience (especially if they *don't* have television or film stars attached). That's just as clear.

Some years ago, Rajiv Joseph's powerful drama *Bengal Tiger at the Baghdad Zoo* opened on Broadway. How did this occur? By casting the late comedic actor Robin Williams. Unfamiliar with the play, some audience members were dismayed to discover that instead of an outrageous comedy with Robin Williams playing a tiger, they were confronted with a play occupied by the ghosts of innocent victims of the Iraq war. Was this an odd casting choice? You bet. Did it help sell tickets? You better believe it.

---

[2]From *Worstward Ho.*

Meanwhile, Lynn Nottage's play *Ruined*, possibly the most important and viscerally moving play in a decade, could not move to Broadway since there was no clear "leading role" that a star could play. I'm not saying this is right or wrong; this is theatrical economics—which has little in common with "success" or "failure." And one flop doesn't make you a failure as a playwright, any more than one hit makes you a success. I repeat—these are meaningless words.

Getting Back on the Horse

My own play was a flop in New York, but I still had confidence in my writing. I couldn't believe that I was a good writer in Chicago, and a lousy writer in Manhattan. So with new determination, I used the invaluable resources of the Playwrights' Center, pulling together some actors to incubate a few new scripts out of the public eye. And I began to develop a new skill—the skill of self-criticism. With observation and concentration, I learned how to be my own toughest critic. I learned the exhilarating art of rewriting. I had discovered that there were plenty of people out there who were all too willing to mess with my work, consciously or unconsciously, and other people who were waiting to judge the results. So I figured out how to beat them to the punch. I learned how—without any need for critical input, only a need to hear the play read out loud—to restructure my scripts, rearrange or even cut scenes if required, and how to throw out apparently wonderful dialogue if it impeded the play. In the process, I developed a keener awareness of the kind of writing I was good at, and the kind of writing I enjoyed. In short, I was developing my "voice."

The truth is, nobody knows what a new play might be, can be, or will be. It takes time to write it, it takes time to hear it, it takes time to rewrite it, and it takes time to rehearse it. And when you reach the first preview performance, not one person—yourself, the director, the actors, the producers—will be able to predict the audience's response.

The audience *makes* the play. It's nothing without them, and everything when they're in the house. And when they're present, responding with tears, laughter, anger, or boredom, then and only then will you begin to understand whether your play works at all. Does your play work? The audience will let you know. Period.

Emerging and Established Playwrights

Believe it or not, I have strong words of encouragement for beginning playwrights. I'll be honest enough to admit I get a little jealous—because the prospects for "emerging" playwrights are enviable. Producers and theaters are actively searching for them—more than any other demographic that exists. That term, "emerging playwright," is a popular one nowadays; it's a birthing term, referring to a writer whose reputation is on the brink of discovery. Quite so—it's often easier to get noticed at the very start of one's writing career. More experienced playwrights often feel like the grown kid in the room who is ignored while everyone coos over the newborn baby.

Still, beginning playwrights tend to be apprehensive. I know a lot of playwrights (both "emerging" and established) who introduce their work with extreme self-deprecation, but it's obviously a preemptive way to ward off criticism. Remember the Hemingway quote? "The first draft of anything is shit." When my students finish their practiced monologues about how terrible their new pages are, I always say the same thing: "Of course they are. Now let's make them better." It's a relief to them—and to me, and to every other working playwright—not to have to prove their "talent" in a first draft. It's very freeing, and allows the writer to focus on the work ahead.

It's important for any playwright to divest themselves of **!**
attitudes that can hinder or cripple their writing.

Try to avoid obsessing on the following questions, which are useless when writing a first draft of *anything*:

a "Is this any good?"

b "Is this better than my last play?"

c "Will the critics like it?" (Ugh.)

d "Am I a better writer than _____" (fill in the blank with whichever playwright is currently receiving media attention)?

e "Will I impact society (or change the world)"?

f "Will this make me famous, or rich, or change my life?"

You get the idea. These obsessions—which have nothing to do with the script itself—only get in the way of progress, and often can lead to "writers' block."

The Next Play

Over the next few years after the *Losing It* trauma, I managed to churn out some plays that had well-received productions in theaters in Minneapolis and St. Paul. But those productions weren't enough for me to make a living. I was broke—seriously broke. This was the Reagan era, a time marked by increasing awareness of the gap between the rich and the poor, the advantaged and the downtrodden. Our political leaders, rather than acknowledging this gap and trying to bridge it, seemed determined to take the path of least resistance, alarmingly exacerbating this social problem (little did I know that by the twenty-first century, these financial and social divides would multiply tenfold, and that Ronald Reagan would appear to be a political moderate in retrospect!).

So I wrote a play about two ex-cons trying to go straight in a world that didn't want them. *T Bone N Weasel* was the fastest play I ever wrote (first draft in three weeks), and to date remains my most frequently produced work. I also challenged myself with a task; I was curious to see if I could write a play with no stage directions, so that's what I did. That may explain its popularity with directors and designers, since they have the freedom to stage my play any way they want to. I give no suggestions.

The production history of this play, especially in its earliest stages, may be instructive. I had learned some lessons from my previous experience, which I was able to apply to its professional development. They paid off.

After my fast first draft, I understood I needed to hear this play out loud, since I was being pretty specific with dialects and cadences. I gathered up some friends to read it at the Playwrights' Center, and since they've never got enough credit for the development of this script, I want to do so now by stating their names: James Williams, who went on to be a frequent actor in the plays of August Wilson; Tim Danz, who now teaches in St. Paul; and Julian Bailey, a hilarious and chameleonic actor who died too young at age 60. These remarkable actors allowed me to see how well the play worked—and the places where it didn't.

A point worth repeating here: arrange to hear your play out loud, at the completion of the first draft. Until then, it's all a guess. With accomplished actors (those who are experienced at the art of the cold reading, a very important and specific skill), you'll be able to more quickly determine whether your play works. If it doesn't, *do not* blame the actors—the responsibility is yours, and yours alone, to make it work better.

With confidence from a successful reading, I submitted the play to PlayLabs and it was accepted. Sounds easy, doesn't it? Well, I'll be honest with you. It *was* a bit easier at that time to have plays accepted into developmental programs; there was less competition. Why? There were simply fewer aspiring playwrights back in the 1980s and 1990s. As Mac Wellman (a fellow playwright and playwriting professor, who started out about the same time I did) said to me a few years ago, "There are so *many* now." Who knew?

For PlayLabs, I was able to procure the talents of the same three actors I had used at the Playwrights' Center, and my friend Steven Dietz took the reins as director. The final staged reading went very well, and I was lucky that some influential theatre folk happened to be in the audience. That led to other productions.

Luck. I'm amazed that I haven't used that word more often by now. So now I'll devote the next chapter to it.

Points to Remember

- "Success" and "Failure" are meaningless words, except in terms of financial impact. So begin to view everything that happens to you as learning experiences, and preparation for the next step.
- After any experience with a play, be sure to take the time to consider what you've learned about your own writing, and developing your own "voice." Apply those discoveries to the development of your next work.
- Take solace in your status as an "emerging" playwright— you're in the most desired group!
- Don't let negativity or overconfidence interfere with your ability to see your own work objectively.
- Learn to enjoy rewriting—by far the best part of writing a play!

9 **Lessons of Luck**

What's Luck Got To Do with It?

More than you might think. Luck is certainly as essential as talent, determination, fortitude, or the willingness to sacrifice. Then how do you encourage good luck or prevent bad luck? You can't. All you can do is be ready for it when it happens.

Good Luck

Let's start with an example of one happy string of good luck. Due to the ongoing interest in my work by the Artistic Director of Seattle's A Contemporary Theatre, Jeff Steitzer, I was fortunate enough to be commissioned to write a stage adaptation of one of my favorite novels: Stendhal's *The Red and the Black*. Fortunately, he liked the adaptation enough to produce it. With additional luck, that production coincided with the Seattle Film Festival. And by lucky coincidence, that book was also the favorite novel of one of the directors premiering a movie there—Taylor Hackford, director of *An Officer and a Gentleman, Ray, The Devil's Advocate*, and many other A-list films. My string of good luck culminated when Hackford came to see the production of my play while he was in town—and lucky for me, he liked it.

I did not engineer any of those events, nor did I have any control over them. That's a sequence determined by sheer luck—and it wasn't even over.

As a result of seeing the Stendhal adaptation, Hackford offered me a writing job, doing the screenplay for a new film based on a short treatment by Billy Bob Thornton. Next came the decision whether to stay at my current temp job, or to quit that and take a short-term writing job that would be the equivalent of six months' salary. As you might imagine, it was a pretty easy decision for me to make.

Before I knew it, I was staying in a guest bedroom at his house in the Hollywood Hills. Having been given the run of the house, one evening I went down to the kitchen to grab myself a snack, and found a woman with her head in the refrigerator, apparently with the same idea. She was slightly startled when she heard me come into the room, and I was significantly more startled to discover that it was Taylor's wife, actress Helen Mirren. Rather than running to the phone to report the strange intruder in her house, she cocked her head and asked me who I was. I replied, "I'm Jon Klein, and I'm writing a movie for your husband." She smiled and calmly said, "Of course you are. Enjoy your stay." I immediately nodded and returned to my room—forgetting the snack, of course. But what difference did that make? I had just been welcomed by Helen Mirren!

I returned to Seattle within the week, and set to work on the screenplay. It involved a few drafts, but Taylor and I were ultimately pleased with the results. I guess you could say my luck ended when he shopped it to a few studios, and they all passed on the project. But that's a matter of odds more than luck, since rejection is the standard and expected response to movie scripts.

According to the WGA, approximately 50,000 items are registered each year—but only a little over a hundred film scripts are actually produced in the same period. That's around one-fifth of one percent, if you don't feel like doing the depressing math yourself. Nonetheless, many screenwriters make a good living writing and polishing movie scripts that will never see the light of day, and I happily joined that club for a short while. And I had great fun doing it. Not only that, it led to another one of my plays being optioned for a film (that didn't get produced either, but who cares?).

I may sound like I'm bragging, but I have a point to make.

When a playwright enters the public arena—with a workshop, a reading, or a full production—it's more likely for good luck to fall in his or her lap. The trick is to keep your lap clear. Be ready for opportunities, and don't be hesitant to grab them when they come your way.

Sometimes you will be required to change your life in a significant way, such as quitting a job or moving to a new town. Of course, you will need to weigh the consequences against your own personal situation. But don't let your choices become determined by hesitancy or fear. Ask questions of others, and especially of yourself. Søren Kierkegaard proclaimed that God's existence cannot be proved; I would maintain that the same is true with the concept of "success," especially in the context of theatre. Sometimes—to use Kierkegaard's famous phrase—it will indeed take a "leap of faith"[1] to accept the risk and see what happens. Be ready for it!

More Good Luck

That leads me to another example of outstanding luck—a production of one of my plays that I had absolutely nothing to do with. I kept hearing about a production of *T Bone N Weasel* at the Alliance Theatre in Atlanta. The play had been directed by a young man named Kenny Leon, and the production sold out to the extent that it moved over to a commercial house, the Academy Theatre, for an open-ended run. The Artistic Director of the Alliance, Bob Farley, called me about his interest in *Southern*

---

[1] Actually not quite correct; his exact phrase was a "leap *to* faith," which is perhaps more helpful.

Cross, a new play I had just premiered at the Illusion Theater in Minneapolis. He invited me to come down and see what was going on with *T Bone N Weasel*, and I gladly accepted the invitation.

It was extraordinarily lucky for me that Kenny was chosen to direct that play, and a good thing for him too—it was one of his first plays at the Alliance, where he was Artistic Associate, and two years later, Artistic Director of the theater. (Since then, he has directed several shows on Broadway, including the recent *Raisin in the Sun* with Denzel Washington, for which Kenny received a Tony Award.)

Kenny's take on my play was astonishingly simple, yet completely original. You may remember that I included no stage directions in the play, which consists of three actors (one of whom plays nine separate characters). Kenny's solution was to have no scenic design; nothing on stage but three chairs, and every single prop was completely mimed. The multi-role actor (Tom Key) was allowed one visual accessory, and one only, to define each new character as he (or she, depending on the moment) appeared. It was an exciting, rowdy show, and purely theatrical. Even the *sports* writer of the Atlanta newspaper wrote a long column about it, stating that my play was even better than the monster truck show that had just come to town.

My luck was compounded by city geography. Both the Alliance Theatre (and the Academy Theatre, a few blocks away) lay across the interstate from a major entertainment outlet: Turner Broadcasting, where the cable networks TNT and TBS had their headquarters, under the leadership of media mogul Ted Turner. Once the folks at Turner heard about the show, they could literally walk across the bridge over to see my show (though I suspect they drove).

I was also lucky that this occurred during a brief period in which Turner Broadcasting was very interested in doing filmed versions of stage plays (including ones by David Mamet, Arthur Miller, and Horton Foote). So it wasn't a completely outrageous notion that they would want to produce my script as a cable movie. I was hired to do the adaptation, and from everything I've learned since, I was treated much more respectfully than most first-time scribes on a film.

I was especially fortunate in being able to work with the late great actor and dancer Gregory Hines. Gregory was especially friendly and gregarious on location, spending time with the local children whose play was being interrupted, or the barber whose shop was temporarily occupied by a film crew.

After a few days there, my presence seemed unnecessary, and I returned to my home in Seattle until the rough cut was ready and I flew back down to Los Angeles. Again, I was treated very generously on that visit. I was even allowed to offer my two cents about the rough cut, and the director, Lewis Teague, was gracious enough to take my suggestion about restoring the play's ending to the film.

During production, whether it's on stage, film or television, don't be too shy about expressing your opinions. Others may add things to your script you didn't expect, but you're still the utmost authority, and should be treated as such. Don't be hesitant just because you're working at a bigger theater, or on a film shoot. You may not win every fight regarding your material, but you should win respect for standing up for yourself. If you work with people who are secure and experienced, you'll achieve that respect.

All in all, the Atlanta experience was a series of very fortunate events, beginning with a novel approach to a play by a young director with a brilliant future, which led directly to a film on a leading cable station. The film was not exactly the play, but millions of people got to see it that would never be able to see it as a stage play, much less ever had the opportunity to see it live. And it was reviewed well, particularly by *Time* magazine and the *Los Angeles Times*. That was pure luck, too (as all good reviews are).

Bad Luck

Sometimes there are events that begin as moments of good luck, but don't pan out as expected. Such was my experience pitching a new show to a major television network. Nowadays playwrights are often sought after by networks and cable channels, since they excel when it comes to character development and interesting dialogue. We're actually living in a renaissance period for writers who travel between the stage and the TV screen. But that was less prevalent in the 1990s, when the network called me in for a meeting to pitch possible television projects. Once again, that call was sheer luck.

I thought I was completely prepared for the meeting, by sending in a full treatment for a new series in advance of my arrival. I had labored over this idea for weeks. And when I had made myself comfortable in their offices, they launched right into their responses to my idea. To my ears, it seemed I had done well. "We've never seen a proposal like this before." "I don't think there's ever been anything on TV quite like this." "This is a very bold, original idea." I started mentally patting myself on my own back, believing my idea was a fait accompli. Where would I live? Manhattan or Hollywood?

"So . . . we hope you'll understand that we're going to pass." Wait a minute. *What?* They were informing me—in the nicest, most respectful way possible—that television required shows that seemed a lot like *other* shows. Familiarity was the key . . . with a slight twist of originality, of course. "What else do you have?" they asked. I was stunned: I had prepared absolutely nothing else—nothing! I had put every available egg from my imagination into one very small basket. Here's the lesson:

Luck alone won't get things done.

You have to be prepared—first of all for luck when it comes your way, but even more importantly to respond to that luck without arrogance, assumptions, or expectations. Remember that being hired to be a dramatic writer means having the ability to produce ideas, dialogue, and structure on short notice . . . and to be able to discard it all and change it on even shorter notice. That's why, in a nutshell, television and film pay so much better than theatre. You're not being hired to show brilliance—you're being hired to supply fast results, for orders dictated by those writing the checks. Artistry is certainly respected. But the entertainment industry wants you to be able to create a product they can *sell*.

Life (and Death) Happens

Death has nothing to do with luck, good or bad. You may be familiar with the story of Jonathan Larson, the book writer of the musical *Rent*, who died on the morning of his first Off-Broadway preview. His show lived on, and achieved glory in Tony Awards and the Pulitzer Prize. But death can also bring projects to a halt.

I had been fortunate enough to receive an Alfred P. Sloan Foundation grant for my play *Chance and Necessity*, and was in residence at Ensemble Studio Theater in NYC, to workshop it and have it performed in a staged reading. After rehearsal, the staff kindly offered to introduce me to the Artistic Director of the theater, Curt Dempster. They walked me up the stairs to his office, and as we peeked in his door, saw that he was on the phone. One of the staff shrugged and said, "No matter—you'll catch him tomorrow when he sees your play." That never happened. That same evening, Curt Dempster committed suicide in the privacy of his New York apartment. The next night, the reading went on as scheduled, but probably should have been postponed; I had an audience of five.

Something similar occurred during deliberations to choose a season at Chicago's famed Goodman Theater. I had a new play called *Dimly Perceived Threats to the System*, which was getting a lot of attention around the country, and I was told the Goodman was considering a production. Play choices at the Goodman are often determined by the directors associated with the theater, and my play was being championed by Associate Artistic Director Michael Maggio. Shortly before the season was announced, Michael passed away, the victim of a long battle with lymphoma caused by a lung transplant at a young age. His death at the age of 49 stunned the Chicago theatre community—and naturally ended plans for my play to be produced there. As a result, my play was bounced from the largest theater in Chicago to one of the smallest—the critically acclaimed About Face Theatre (who did a fine job with it).

These were all very sad occasions, for which I could have selfishly cursed my own bad luck—but that would have been appallingly egotistical, since my professional misfortunes were dwarfed by the personal impacts caused by the deaths of these legendary artists. I may have been obliquely affected, and the timing may have been regrettable, but the truth was that these events had *nothing to do with me*. And that's true for luck—good or bad—in general.

It may seem like there's nothing you can do to prepare for bad luck. You may think that it's outside of your control, so it's pointless to try. But I disagree with that.

You *can* prepare yourself for luck when it strikes. That means taking positive steps to send luck your way.

How? The old cliché—being at the right place at the right time. Yes, your control over that may be limited. But if you make yourself ready for opportunities when they arise, you won't be completely thrown. And if bad luck hits you instead, you won't be devastated.

Always be ready for good luck to turn bad, or for bad luck to turn good. The unpredictability of life contributes to an uncertain career in the theater. But with a little forethought and flexibility, you can go with the flow and be prepared for any sudden adjustment. As my experience with that television network showed, it's often important to have a "Plan B."

Points to Remember

- Luck is an uncontrollable but potent factor in playwriting. The truth is, luck is often accompanied by the need to make *decisions* on how to respond to that luck.

- The important thing is to prepare yourself for its vicissitudes, and to take advantage of unexpected fortune.

- The main way a playwright can encourage good luck is to be visible—getting your writing seen, either in development or in production, will increase your chances for good opportunities.

- Film and television work can sometimes come to a playwright out of productions, especially if they're in close proximity to directors and producers actively looking for writers.

- By all means be hopeful for good luck, but don't let bad luck throw you when it happens. Remember that random events may affect your play, but don't let them affect you as a person. They have nothing to do with you!

10 How Other Playwrights Got Started

Introduction

I realize that my own viewpoints and opinions about a life in the theatre are completely subjective and affected by my own personal experience. Much of that experience has been described in this book. But I wanted to give some other personal perspectives, since the journeys taken by playwrights are quite diverse.

So I've asked some other American writers to contribute a few stories of their own. Some of them you may have heard of; some of them you probably haven't. They do represent a broad degree of theatrical experience, from writers just starting to make a name for themselves to seasoned, award-winning veterans. They are all very talented and smart writers who are completely dedicated to their craft. And so they are worth including here, in their own voices, reprinted verbatim.

I asked them all to respond to two questions:

1   **What were the circumstances of your first professional "break," that began your career as a working playwright? To what extent did you make it happen yourself?**

2   **What was your most important decision affecting your own professional career? In hindsight, was it a good decision or not?**

These playwrights enthusiastically responded, sometimes separating the questions, sometimes combining them, sometimes taking detours into other subjects. You'll notice that a lot of them talk about some of the same subjects I spoke of earlier, which is only natural because that's how playwrights think and talk. And you'll see that many of them have spent time at some of the American theaters and developmental programs I have mentioned.

I think their responses provide alternative insights into how to "break in" as a playwright, and the kinds of rewards and obstacles that may be found along the way. Most interesting to me is that without my even asking, they almost all want to talk about "success," and how they've learned to define that word for themselves.

We'll take a look at our guest playwrights alphabetically. I'll repeat those two questions in the first response; afterwards I'll assume you know them.

Stories from 17 Other Dramatists

Sheila Callaghan

Sheila Callaghan's plays have been produced and developed with Soho Rep, Playwright's Horizons, Yale Rep, South Coast Repertory, Clubbed Thumb, The LARK, ATL, New Georges, The Flea, Woolly Mammoth, Boston Court, and Rattlestick Playwright's Theatre, among others. Sheila is the recipient of the Princess Grace Award for emerging artists, a Jerome Fellowship from the Playwright's Center in Minneapolis, a MacDowell Residency, a Cherry Lane Mentorship Fellowship, the Susan Smith Blackburn Award, and the prestigious Whiting Award. Her plays have been produced internationally in New Zealand, Australia, Norway, Germany, Portugal, and the Czech Republic.

Sheila's response:

1 What were the circumstances of your first professional "break," that began your career as a working playwright? To what extent did you make it happen yourself?

Winning the Princess Grace Award. It gave me a one-year residency at New Dramatists, where I got to meet and consort with my heroes. It was open submission. Before then I had been applying for everything, and I mean literally everything. Things I would have no chance at winning because my material wasn't necessarily relevant to the award or theatre. I was told to get my work out there no matter how or where, which was a bad idea. It was a tremendous amount of work. And also, terribly inefficient. Took me a while to figure out that the better idea was to look at the biographies and resumes of the people I admire the most, take note of the kinds of things they had done, the paths they had taken, the theaters and directors and actors they worked with, etc., and model my career after that. That's when things started to gain momentum for me.

2 What was your most important decision affecting your own professional career? In hindsight, was it a good decision or not?

Moving to New York. For me, it was the only decision. I have a community there, I see so much incredible work, and I am inspired on a daily basis by artists and theaters I admire. But it's really, really hard to live there as a family. Recently I've been spending a lot more time in LA to work in television, and while I love LA and feel creatively fulfilled by the material I've been producing, the longer I spend away from my New York home the harder it is for me to continue to make work there. I try to be in both cities at the same time, but I can't feed my kid being a playwright, and there are simply less opportunities for television work in New York. But my time spent seeing/making theatre in New York continues to shape my aesthetic and inform my identity as a playwright. Having an artistic home is so important to me. Maybe even essential.

Allyson Currin

Allyson Currin is the author of over thirty plays including the recent world premiere of her new musical *Silver Belles* at Tony Award-winning Signature Theatre (with Matt Conner and Stephen Gregory Smith) and the world premiere of her new play *Sooner/Later* at Cincinnati Playhouse (directed by Wendy Goldberg). Other plays of hers have premiered at The John F. Kennedy Center for the Performing Arts, Imagination Stage, WSC Avant Bard, Pinky Swear Productions, Cincinnati Playhouse, Source Theatre Company, Doorway Arts Ensemble, American Century Theatre, The National Museum for Women in the Arts, Charter Theatre, and The Strathmore, among others.

Allyson's response:

1   I didn't start out as a playwright. I was a professional actor and director who wrote non-theatrical literature for fun. I wrote my first one-act on a whim. Showed it to a theatre festival director on a whim. On a whim, he said, "Let's do a 10-minute version of it for the Festival." So I did. An artistic director saw it and asked for a full copy of the script, and that's how it got produced. That premiere was the best night of my life, because I realized FOR THE FIRST TIME that being a playwright was what I was really supposed to be doing in theatre. That was twenty-five years ago and I haven't stopped writing for a minute since. But when I think back to the unconsidered way I found playwriting, it terrifies me because it was such a near miss. . . . And although my first production was a happy accident, nothing else about my career has been. I have been working, promoting, networking, shopping scripts around, riding various development wheels, succeeding and failing with regularity the entire time. It's tough work. If you have talent and you stick with it, it can be done. But the profession is not for those who are unwilling to take a lot of hits.

2 I definitely reached a point in my playwriting career when I had to learn to say no to certain work. Being something of a "good girl" and a people-pleaser, that was a hard lesson to learn. But you do reach a point when you have to decline opportunities from perfectly well-intentioned people, when you as a writer have grown past them. I do not work for free. I have turned down jobs that I felt were for "emerging" playwrights, once I considered myself "established." It always gives me a stomach ache to say no to anyone, of course (there is a deep-seated fear that ALL the opportunities will dry up and you'll never work again). But you do reach a point where certain jobs are, pardon the snobbery of the phrase, beneath you. I had to work hard to learn to value my playwriting, as both art and commodity. To respect my craft enough to learn to say no, when appropriate, was a huge milestone in my growth as a playwright. And the good news is that this attitude towards my work has elevated my profile regionally and nationally.

Steven Dietz

Steven Dietz's plays and adaptations have been seen at over one hundred regional theatres in the United States, as well as Off-Broadway and internationally. Dietz received the Steinberg New Play Citation for *Bloomsday* (having also been a finalist for *Becky's New Car* and *Last of the Boys*); the PEN USA West Award for *Lonely Planet*; and the Kennedy Center Fund for New American Plays award for both *Still Life with Iris* and *Fiction* (produced Off-Broadway by the Roundabout Theatre Company). Recent premieres include *This Random World* (2016 Humana Festival of New American Plays), *On Clover Road* (NNPN Rolling World Premiere), and *Rancho Mirage* (Edgerton New Play Award). Dietz teaches playwriting and directing at the University of Texas at Austin.

Steven's response:

1 My first major professional break came about 7 years into my professional career. I had had a few plays produced in Minneapolis (where I was living), but then a Minneapolis director who had moved to Seattle introduced me and my work to ACT Theatre in Seattle. This led to a commission of my play, *God's Country*. That was the play that suddenly opened numerous regional (and even NYC) doors for me.

I only made this happen in the sense that I continued to make work and write plays for my community in Minneapolis, and I spoke openly and avidly of further plays I hoped to create. My relationship with this director (David Ira Goldstein)—begun in Minneapolis—blossomed in Seattle with this commission of *God's Country* (which David Ira directed), and led to many more premieres at ACT Theatre. This was sublime good fortune, but I'd like to think it also was connected to my demonstrated practice of delivering the plays that I had promised.

2 By far the biggest decision of my career was to move from Minneapolis (where not only ALL my best friends lived, but where I had a long history as a playwright and director) to Seattle—where I knew almost no one . . . but there was a theatre that had committed to my work. I had no idea—nor any promise whatsoever—that they (ACT Theatre) would commit to anything beyond the one play they had commissioned; nor did I have any connection to another theatre in that city. I had put too many eggs in one basket.

But, as it happened, the relationship flourished. And something more: I discovered that sometimes you are not able/meant to practice your craft in the same place where you have learned your craft. The challenge of my writing deepened when I moved to Seattle. And that was good for me. My plays are the traces of my life—and those traces now include my home of Denver, my artistic journeys in Minneapolis and Seattle, and my current home in Austin, TX.

Robert Freedman

Robert L. Freedman won Tony, Drama Desk, and Outer Critics Circle Awards for Best Book of a Musical for *A Gentleman's Guide to Love and Murder*, the 2014 Best Musical Tony winner. He was also nominated for a Tony for Best Score with composer and co-lyricist Steven Lutvak, with whom he shared the 2014 Drama Desk Award for Best Lyrics, a 2015 Grammy nomination, and the Kleban and Fred Ebb awards. For his television work, Robert won the Writers Guild Award for HBO's *A Deadly* Secret, and was nominated for an Emmy Award and a Writers Guild Award for the miniseries *Life With Judy Garland: Me and My Shadows*.

Robert's response:

After graduating from college, where I received a BA in Theatre and where four of my one-act plays were produced, I worked for a year as a word processor for an entertainment law firm in Los Angeles. During that year, I began to lose my identity as a writer. I was invited to a dinner party by a friend, not knowing that an important producer was going to be there. When asked, "What do you do, Robert?" I answered, "I'm a word processor at a law firm." My friend was surprised and elbowed me, "Tell him, Robert! You're a writer!" I had really kind of forgotten. During that year at the law firm, I saw young men not much older than me proudly brandishing the accoutrements of success—three-piece suits, sports cars, a superior attitude. As if to show them, I applied to law school myself. At the same time, I applied to a new graduate program at NYU in Dramatic Writing. I got into both. The chairman of the department at NYU called me to urge me to come east. She said, "If you really want to be a writer, you're going to have to come to New York eventually." That was all I needed to hear. Someone giving me permission to think of myself as a writer, and to avoid the "safe" route of law school. I've never looked back.

Gary Garrison

For the last decade, Gary Garrison was the executive director of the DGA—the national organization of playwrights, lyricists, and composers headed by our nation's most honored dramatists. Prior to his work at the Guild, Garrison filled the posts of artistic director, producer, and full-time faculty member in the Goldberg Department of Dramatic Writing at NYU's Tisch School of the Arts, where he produced over forty-five different festivals of new work, collaborating with hundreds of playwrights, directors, and actors. In the spring of 2016, he was awarded the Milan Stitt Outstanding Teacher of Playwriting by the Kennedy Center.

Gary's response:

The world is tiny-tiny. And the world of theater is obviously even smaller. Everybody knows everybody in some form or fashion; we're all interconnected in ways we discover daily. Just when you think you can hide, someone says from the dark, "Oh, I know you. We met in . . . ." It's all to say, then, that I learned early on that I better remember to always put my best foot forward, to look someone in the eye when I met them, to speak about my work only in the most positive terms (and not sound like a critic of my own career), to share what I have with other people, to be inquisitive about others as much as I was about my own future and to learn to listen attentively and care passionately about my journey. I knew early on that I needed to be a good citizen of my community, and as importantly, a good citizen in my own heart for myself. With all of that in play, I have to say a lot of good opportunities came to me instead of me being in constant state of pursuit. I was very fortunate. I mean, yes, I'm talented. But in this day and age, that will get you about halfway there. You also have to look like someone that people want to be close to, as opposed to avoiding like a platter of bad lasagna.

Keith Glover

Keith Glover is the author of *Dancing on Moonlight* which was produced at the Joseph Papp Public Theater by the New York Shakespeare Festival. His second play, *Coming of the Hurricane*, premiered at the Denver Center Theater Company and at the Crossroads Theater Company with Viola Davis. His Streetbeat Bopera *In Walks Ed*, directed by Mr. Glover was the recipient of the Rosenthal Prize and subsequently nominated for the Pulitzer Prize for drama. Mr. Glover is the writer of the 234th edition of *Ringling Bros.*, and *Barnum and Bailey, The Greatest Show on Earth* which subsequently toured the world.

Keith's response:

1 When I was starting out the costs were enormous with the hard copying of scripts and the mailing of them. From the very start I set up a system to flag the theaters which I believed would be receptive to what I was writing at the time and which weren't. So that allowed me to shape my initial interactions from the beginning. It doesn't make sense to send your play to a theater that doesn't share your aesthetic. I didn't have an agent and I didn't have any credits. I also was very big on competitions which helped me to move from draft to draft. If there was a contest deadline that I was interested in entering, I would focus on completing a new draft by that deadline. My break came at the Denver Center which selected my play, *Coming of The Hurricane*, to be a part of their winter festival of readings through an open submission. I still didn't have an agent or credits. I met a great director, Israel Hicks, who taught me more in those two weeks about writing than anyone then or since. I came back to NY and sat for weeks waiting and then received the call that they were going to produce the play in their upcoming season! Finally the struggle is over! They sent me a contract and asked that I give it to my agent. I didn't have one! So I called a bunch of agents. I said, "I need somebody to negotiate this contract so I don't get screwed and I'll give you the commission. No strings and you don't have to represent me after." Every agent on my list rejected me cold without even reading anything. I had to call the theater and ask for help and they gave my script to a young agent named Bruce Ostler to read. He read it over the weekend called me on Monday and said he wanted to represent me. Two days later, George C. Wolfe called from the NY Shakespeare Festival and said he wanted to produce my first play, *Dancing on Moonlight*. The next week I was in a blurb in the *New York Times* and every agent that rejected me called me back wanting to represent me. I am still with Bruce and we've been together for over twenty years and counting.

2 I think it's very easy to be seduced by critical attention and success early in your career. It's very easy to be put into a box that announces what kind of work that you do and the kind of stories that the community can come to you to provide. This I believe is anathema to growth as an artist. Because if you're lucky after your breakthrough you will have those discussions about where to go next, what to write next, what you're interested in. The media is also very good about putting you in a box especially after a hit. I observed that a great many critics like to claim ownership over a writer and their work, especially if they have praised them in the past or were instrumental in their break. They can be very vindictive if the subsequent work isn't in the same vein or direction they have praised previously, which can wreak havoc to the prospects of the new play and your career momentum. I was presented with this right after I broke through with my musical *Thunder Knocking on the Door*, which was a huge hit regionally and I was under a lot of pressure to write a follow up folksy musical which would have the reputation of *Thunder* and that was the last thing I wanted to do. I followed it up with a Vampire Western, *Dark Paradise,* and I really got creamed for it and fell off the radar. I expected it and pressed on anyway. I had to grow comfortable with the notion of wandering in the wilderness, which meant to me writing what I wanted to write and being okay, if I didn't have a bunch of co-productions lined up, if any productions at all. It was very liberating. It made me a very dangerous person with a pen.

Allison Gregory

Allison Gregory's plays have been produced all over the country and she has received commissions, grants, and development from Oregon Shakespeare Festival, South Coast Repertory, ACT, The Kennedy Center, Hedgebrook, New Harmony, and many others. Her work has been the recipient of the Julie Harris Playwriting Award, South Coast Repertory Theatre's Playwrights Award, Garland & Dramalogue Awards. Her plays include *Not Medea* (O'Neill finalist, NNPN Rolling World Premieres); *Motherland* (O'Neill finalist; American Blues Award finalist; NNPN Showcase selection); and *Wild Horses* (NNPN Rolling World Premieres). allisongregoryplays.com

Allison's response:

1 I write for adults and I write for young audiences, two sadly and strangely unrelated theatre worlds, so my break came in two stages. I had written my first play (for grownups) in a workshop at South Coast Repertory, taught by two terrific dudes: Richard Hellesen initially and then John Glore. I'd never taken a playwriting course, but I'd acted in several new plays; I was curious and blessedly oblivious. Also I was inspired by a hard crush on a certain playwright who later became my husband . . . but that's its own play.

The one I wrote—on a Brother GX-6750 Daisy electronic typewriter—was titled *Forcing Hyacinths*. I submitted it to SCR for their no-longer existing California Playwright's Competition, and to the Julie Harris Playwright Award Competition. Winning has never been as easy since: I suddenly had a commission from SCR and award money from the Julie Harris people, and interest in my work. After years of struggling as an actor this playwriting thing was so easy!

That is called luck. Because really I had no skill, no craft, and only a sprinkling of talent. It's no recipe for sustained success, but I give myself big props for diving in and for putting it out there before I knew what I was doing. There's an energy to those early initiatives that you gotta respect.

My launch into theatre for youth was initiated by the wonderful David Saar, Artistic Director/Playwright at Childsplay, Inc. I had heard such great things about him and shyly sent him my first children's play, *Even Steven Goes to War*. We were taking a road trip down the coast when I got the call that he wanted to take the play to the Kennedy Center for New Visions/New Voices. He produced the play within the year. I can't thank him enough for believing deeply that a play about the Vietnam War could be suitable for children. He is still my hero.

2 I can't say there was any single important decision. Honestly? It's been series of steps and missteps, all of them necessary for my own personal trajectory. I began playwriting late, after careers as a dancer and then an actor. I soaked things up as I went along and learned the ropes en route. If forced to pin it down . . . I would say the most important decision was sitting down that first time with the intention to write. And then finding the willing person who would read what I wrote.

Lauren Gunderson

Lauren Gunderson is the most-produced living playwright in America in 2017. She is the winner of the Lanford Wilson Award and the Steinberg/ATCA New Play Award, a finalist for the Susan Smith Blackburn Prize and John Gassner Award for Playwriting, and a recipient of the Mellon Foundation's 3-Year Residency with Marin Theatre Co. Her work has been commissioned, produced, and developed at companies across the United States, including South Cost Rep, The Kennedy Center, The O'Neill, The Denver Center, Oregon Shakespeare Festival, Berkeley Rep, Marin Theatre, Synchronicity, and more. Her work is published by Playscripts, Dramatists Play Service, and Samuel French.

Lauren's response:

1 I started writing quite young and the only thing I knew to do with the plays I wrote was to send them to contests I found looking through *The Dramatists Sourcebook* from the Dramatists Guild. My first full-length play, which I wrote at 17, was a story of a family of Southern women and most of it was set inside a Winnebago. I really didn't understand the rules of writing yet and if I was abiding them or breaking them. So I gave it to a theatre director, Peter Hardy, who had started Essential Theatre in Atlanta. I'd been in a play that he produced as an actor and asked him if he would look at the play and tell me if I'd actually written one or not. He read it and said that, yes, it was a play and that he'd like to award it the Essential Theatre prize for best new play by a Georgia writer. I was pretty damn stunned. Peter's company produced the play as part of the award, and that's how my very first production manifested. But what is very clear to me in retrospect was the value of getting something down on the page and getting it out there. If I'd have kept that play to myself and was afraid to show anyone until I knew it was a perfect thing I might never have become a playwright. Also this confirmed to me that you don't need to have your first break in New York or Chicago to start a real career in theatre. Experiences and people and lessons I learned working in my hometown continue to define me and my career now.

2 In 2009 I moved from New York City to San Francisco because I fell in love. With the city, with a man, with a community of artists. At once it felt both completely right and also completely against the path I'd been following so far. I'd moved to NYC to study at NYU's Tisch School, I was ready to become a New Yorker after graduating, I was committed to trying to be a professional playwright and here I was moving to the opposite side of the country from the epicenter of American theatre. But that move opened up my career in ways I couldn't have predicted. To begin with I was brought to SF to workshop a new play with Marin Theatre Company and Jasson Minadakis. While in SF for that development process I met my future husband as well as a community of truly gifted theatre artists. I found that San Francisco is new play town. The amount of theatre companies is large and diverse. The amount of productions (not just readings and workshops) of new plays is large and diverse. This town likes art and novelty and innovation. Also it's gorgeous and the food is really good.

When I moved officially to San Francisco I immediately reached out to theatre community leaders (Amy Mueller at Playwrights Foundation, Marissa Wolf and Crowded Fire Theatre, the playwrights Peter Nachtrieb and Octavio Solis) and started to find a community. A few years later I had five new plays premiering at five different theaters in the Bay Area in one year. That's crazy. But it proves that I'd found a city where the variety of my writing can find a variety of homes. I'd found my people. I'd found where I can work the way I like to work. I'd found a place where I could grow. The amount of rehearsal and work and collaboration let me get better as a writer. And those plays that started here in SF have flown all over the country and seen multiple productions and publication. In fact my first off-Broadway production came to NYC as a transfer from San Francisco Playhouse. And the actors that I have met here in Bay Area have become my cohorts. I write for them and get the pleasure of thinking of the Bay Area as a kind of repertory. Some of those actors have gone with plays of mine to other cities too.

I am sure that, by leaving NYC, I gave up opportunities and relationships that would have certainly influenced my career. And I miss New York. I miss the shows and the people and the energy of it. But San Francisco gave me a deep well of inspiration, relationships and opportunity to not just write but to develop and produce my work (and myself). I would never have had that many productions in that amount of time in New York, and many of those plays may have faded away.

I didn't plan for the Bay Area to be the career crucible that it turned out to be. But a decision that I originally made for love and curiosity (and more than a little of "oh what the hell") became a decision that let my writing and career find room, support and fertilizer to thrive. The lesson for me is: follow your curiosity, your happiness, your (I know this is cheesy) heart, not just your career. And when you find it? Write like mad.

Chad Henry

Chad Henry is an actor, playwright, lyricist, composer, and novelist, with over twenty musical theatre titles to his credit. He coauthored, with A. M. Collins, the long-running rock musical *Angry Housewives*, which played for seven years in Seattle, and went on to be produced around the world and almost adapted for the movies. Henry also has written some dozen original musicals for Seattle Children's Theatre, including *Little Lulu, The Magic Mrs. Piggle Wiggle,* and *Good Night Moon*. His musicals for young audiences have been produced nationally at leading US children's theaters, and published with Samuel French, DPS, PYA, and others. His YA (young adult) novel, *Dogbreath Victorious*, has been published by Holiday House.

Chad's response:

While trying for an acting career in Seattle in the 1970s and '80's, I found myself inexplicably being asked to write songs for new shows for Seattle area theatres, initially Empty Space theatre. I was called to write songs for a production of *The Venetian Twins*, directed by actor John Aylward. In the cast was actor-director John Kauffman, who later directed several more original musical theatre adaptations for Seattle's Empty Space, many of them outdoor park productions, and Johnny brought me in to write music and lyrics for each show he directed. Later on, director Linda Hartzell, a college friend, was putting together a team to create an original musical for Pioneer Square Theatre, to be called *Angry Housewives*, with a book by Annamarie Collins, one of the artistic directors of Pioneer Square, a theatre which at that time was financially in the hole. Hartzell convinced Ms. Collins to bring me in to write the songs. *Housewives*, a show produced on the most frayed of shoestrings, turned out to be a huge hit, running for seven years in Seattle alone, and later also Off-Broadway, all over the US and Canada, and in Europe, Asia, and Australia.

Shortly after, director Linda Hartzell was hired to run Seattle Children's Theatre, and she asked me to write a show for her theatre, which I did. This was the first time I wrote a complete script, albeit an adaptation, as well as music and lyrics. Over the years, Ms. Hartzell commissioned at least ten musical theatre scripts from me, many of which have had national productions, including my latest, an adaptation of the picture book *Good Night Moon*. Writing for children's theatre was not a goal I imagined for myself, but at least SCT had very high production standards, using adult Equity actors in all cases, and paid reasonably well for the amount of time and work. Because almost all of these shows, at Ms. Hartzell's request, were adaptations, the royalty split was not always the greatest, although I have had a couple of scripts published as a result. Many of my commissions were odd ones, including writing music and lyrics for Cornish School's senior production of Johann Nestroy's *Love Affairs and Wedding Bells*, originally to be directed by John Kauffman, but who was replaced on John's death by Edward Payson Call, and featuring graduating actor Brendan Fraser. Call was one of the very best directors I've ever worked with, and was instrumental in improving my song lyrics. One other adult musical that I was brought into by Ms. Hartzell, was a musical eventually titled *Labor of Love*, which was a collaboration between Seattle's One-Reel Productions, and a Japanese theatre company called Furusato Caravan. I co-wrote the book and music and lyrics with the

Japanese artistic team. This show toured throughout Japan and the US, and played the Olympics Arts Festival in Barcelona.

My career as a writer was a kind of odd track, since almost all my significant work has come to me as commissions, and in most cases any original scripts I have written and submitted to various theatres have not been accepted for development or production. When I complained about my failure to have my original work accepted for production Ms. Hartzell suggested I work on "spec" and used playwright Steven Dietz as a model—but it hasn't worked for me. So I would have to say, I am not much of a role model for an aspiring playwright. I never really made an important decision affecting my writing career, other than to stay open to requests to accept commissions. I currently have about five titles—both original and adaptation—that I am working on, but these are all on "spec" and I have no idea if any of them will be accepted anywhere. One of the perks of my so-called career has been the opportunity to travel with these shows to London, Japan, Barcelona, Canada, and throughout the US.

Cory Hinkle

Cory Hinkle was the winner of the 2015 Heideman Award for his play, *This Quintessence of Dust* and he was a co-writer of *That High Lonesome Sound*, both of which premiered at the Humana Festival. His plays *Little Eyes* and *SadGrrl13* premiered at the Workhaus Collective, a company he co-ran with eight other playwrights from 2007 to 2012. His plays have been produced or developed at the Sundance Theatre Lab, Guthrie Theater, The Road Theatre, Moving Arts, Jackalope Theatre, Chalk Rep, The Theatre @ Boston Court, Mixed Blood Theatre, the Bay Area Playwrights Festival, Cape Cod Theater Project, HERE Arts Center, and New York Theatre Workshop, among others.

Cory's response:

1 The single most important moment of my career was receiving the Jerome fellowship at the Playwrights' Center. Up to that point, I knew I wanted to be a playwright, but I didn't know what a career might look like, or if that was even possible. I just knew that I was committed and couldn't really imagine doing anything else. At some point after college, I read *Polaroid Stories* by Naomi Iizuka and loved it. On the back cover it said that Naomi had done a Jerome fellowship at the Playwrights' Center. Based mostly on the fact that one of my favorite writers at that time had done a Jerome fellowship I figured that the Playwrights' Center was the place for me. I started applying and kept applying. I was finally accepted when I was the second alternate on the third time I applied (I mention that because I have rarely received anything in playwriting on the first try). The most significant aspect of the Jerome was that it helped me see what a career as a playwright might look like. I was suddenly surrounded by other writers who were serious about pursuing this as a career.

2 The Jerome fellowship gave me a group of peers; it gave me collaborators; it gave me connections within the industry. Also, I learned a ton from the other writers at the Playwrights' Center. That was the biggest step forward for me—I became a much better writer because of where I was and who I was surrounded by. I was inspired by those other writers; they became my colleagues and we helped each other sustain and build our careers. In fact, many of us went on to form a playwright-driven theatre company called the Workhaus Collective where two of my plays were produced.

Velina Hasu Houston

Velina Hasu Houston is an internationally celebrated writer with over 24 commissions in theatre, musical theatre, and opera. In New York, nationally, and globally, her work has been produced at such theatres as Manhattan Theatre Club, Old Globe Theatre, The Pasadena Playhouse, TheatreWorks, and Theatre X (Tokyo). Honored by the Kennedy Center, Smithsonian Institute, Rockefeller Foundation, Japan Foundation, Wallace Foundation, Doris Duke Charitable Foundation, and others, she founded graduate playwriting studies at the USC School of Dramatic Arts in 1991, where she is a Distinguished Professor of Dramatic Writing, Director of Dramatic Writing, Resident Playwright, and Associate Dean of Faculty.

Velina's response:

1 My first professional break occurred in New York City. The first theatre that treated me honorably and never brought up the issue of my multiethnic background was New York's Manhattan Theatre Club. It focused on the play—my play *Tea*—and, because of that, I consider my experience there as my first professional break. I reflect upon the MTC experience as a starting point because, after its production of *Tea* in 1987, my work began to be produced nationwide and in other countries, thus catapulting my literary career in ways that previous experiences had not. I believe that artists ultimately must make their art live and breathe on their own. That does not mean that certain individuals or organizations do not play a part in that—they most certainly do and I am grateful to all of them—but none of those experiences would happen without an artist first and foremost believing in his or her work and striving to bring it to life via traditional and non-traditional means. In cultivating one's career as a literary artist, speed bumps exist in and of themselves or are placed before you intentionally. The artist's life is not an easy one, but such challenges increase the mettle that must be scraped together with fortitude to help you propel yourself forward. MTC found my play *Tea* via my many efforts to bring attention to the play, which included entering it into competitions. After they produced *Tea*, it came to the attention of the Old Globe Theatre and many other theatres nationwide and globally. My professional career in the theatre began at the age of twenty-three and has sustained with a vigor that continues to surprise me, and which I honor and for which I am grateful. Today, over twenty-five years since *Tea* had its first professional production, it continues to be produced in Asia and the United States; and studied globally including in Egypt, Japan, China, and India.

2 My most important decision affecting my playwriting career involved a commission from a Los Angeles-based theatre. Because I only truly knew one member of the company and therefore had not cultivated relationships of trust with the other company members, I asked if I could create an outline of the desired play and have that read aloud to them. I asked them to approve the outline so that, once the play based on that outline was completed, they could not backslide and say that it was not the play that they desired. My colleague agreed that that method was a good approach. So I outlined the characters and story in detail, and met with the company to have a reading. The company applauded the reading and agreed that the proposed play was precisely what they wanted. So I invested time and energy in creating that play. Once it was completed, the company rejected it, stating that it wanted a different story altogether. I was astonished. But then the company made another request. They asked my agent if the commission money could be refunded. It was my agent's turn to be astonished. My colleague who was a company member apologized, but the company began a rumor mill positioning itself as ethical. Turn of events? The commission money was not refunded. I did not move forward with the company to develop and produce the play that I had written. In fact, I never again worked with the company. Furthermore, I had to cope with vilifying statements made about me by company members. My experience with them taught me a great deal about the nature of commissions. From that point forward, I counseled many student playwrights about the nature of commissions, and advised them to behave ethically and demand ethical treatment. Commissions should be made either for projects that are specific to a company's desires (and so articulated) or should be granted to an artist of the company's choice, entrusting that artist with creating a work of art that reflects the views that the company wanted. Of course, the result can never be all things to all company members, but it can really be something. To behave in any other way is uncivilized and unethical. I do not regret the turn of events. Since that time, I have had twenty-four other commissions.

Meg Maroshnik

Meg Maroshnik is a Los Angeles-based, Minneapolis-bred playwright who writes heightened language. Plays include *The Fairytale Lives of Russian Girls* (Yale Rep; Alliance), *The Tall Girls* (Alliance; O'Neill; La Jolla Playhouse DNA Series), *Fickle: A Fancy French Farce* (Olney Theatre Center), *The Droll* (Pacific Playwrights Festival; Undermain), *Lady Tattoo* (Pacific Playwrights Festival), and *Utopia, Minnesota* (Williamstown Theatre Festival Sagal Fellowship). Awards: Whiting Award, Susan Smith Blackburn finalist, Alliance/Kendeda Graduate Playwriting Award. Publications: Samuel French. MFA: Yale School of Drama under Paula Vogel. Affiliation: Core Writer at the Playwrights' Center and co-founder of the Kilroys.

Meg's responses:

1 When I lived in NYC after college, I spent 90 percent of my time on money/survival work. And then split the remaining 10 percent of my time between sleep and writing plays! All this to say, I didn't write a whole lotta new work in those years. For me, the leap to really making theater came when I went to graduate school. Going to a funded MFA program gave me the time and space to immerse myself in theater full-time. I can trace all of my first professional opportunities to the collaborators and mentors I met in graduate school. And, crucially, my first professional production (*The Fairytale Lives of Russian Girls* at the Alliance Theatre in 2012) came out of the Alliance/Kendeda Graduate Playwriting award, an amazing competition that awards a production to a playwright in their final year of an MFA program.

2 In all honesty, the most important recent decisions that have bled into my professional life have all been personal life ones. My playwriting path over the past couple years has been shaped by the decision to have children—and the decisions that came along with it. I moved to Los Angeles and the way I look at my time and travel shifted entirely. I started doing more advocacy work as a co-founder of the Kilroys. This decision was unquestionably a "good" one for me personally, but I think that, in the middle of it all, it's hard to say how good it will have been for my "career". But living a full life is important to me as a writer, too, so that is what it is!

John Olive

John Olive is a widely produced and award-winning playwright, a novelist, a screenwriter, and a popular teacher of creative writing. John's plays include *Standing On My Knees, Minnesota Moon, The Voice of the Prairie, Evelyn & the Polka King, Killers, The Summer Moon, The Ecstasy of St. Theresa,* and *Careless Love*, among others. Producing theaters include the Manhattan Theatre Club, Old Globe, Steppenwolf, Wisdom Bridge, South Coast Rep, Alley Theater, the Guthrie, ATL, the Oregon Shakespeare Festival, ACT/Seattle, and many others. John has recently published a book, about the magic of bedtime stories: *Tell Me A Story in The Dark*.

John's response:

1   My first "break." This would have to be my one act *Minnesota Moon*. Late 1970s. My first "good" play. I recall that I was driving a cab and while waiting for a fare at the airport I began work on the play. At the time, I was regularly going to New York, to see plays and to imbibe the atmosphere (I was semi-planning to move to the city, which I did, 10 years later, for 7 or 8 months). Anyway, once *Moon* was finished, I travelled now with this play. It attracted the attention of a bona fide literary agent. She set up a reading of the play at Circle Repertory (Lanford Wilson's company). I wasn't there, but because of the reading I received a "firm" offer (I remember this word) from Circle Rep to produce *Minnesota Moon*. They did. The production starred Jeff Daniels. Got a good review in the *Times*. I met the great Lanford Wilson. I was off and running. At the time, I didn't buy a celebratory bottle of wine, anything like that. I just thought, "This is how it's supposed to work. No big deal." What did I do to affect this "break"? I wrote the play. This is the key: work hard. Be talented.

2 My biggest decision? To pursue playwriting at all. At one point, in the late 1980s/early 1990s, I was making good money: plays being produced, grants, Hollywood. I must have said to myself, "Gosh, I think I'll do this. I am doing it. I'll keep on." But I don't remember. I just carried on, more interested in the day-to-day flow of my life than the Future. Was it a good life? It was, and I'm glad I did it. Would I pursue the theater if I had it to do over? I would not! I would do something else. What, I don't know, but . . . something. Now I'm writing books, screenplays, reviews, and, of course, the occasional play. Teaching. I'm a father and husband. (This, by the way, is my best advice: get into a relationship that will sustain you through the myriad ups and downs of the Writer's Life.) My health is reasonably good. I'm happy. Aren't I?

Brendan Pelsue

Actor's theatre credits include *Edge Play* and *Cabin Fever* (Apprentice/Intern Tens).

Other theatre: *Hagoromo*, Brooklyn Academy of Music; *Parking Lot*, Riverbank and *Varieties of Religious Experience* (upcoming) at Yale School of Drama; *Read to Me* (workshop), Bay Area Playwrights Festival; *Ecology of a Visit*, Corkscrew Theater Company; *Petra and the Saints*, Telephonic Literary Union; *Diagram of a Kidnapping*, Brown University New Plays Festival; and *Millyard*, MA, Firehouse Center for the Arts. Pelsue holds a BA from Brown University and is an MFA student at Yale School of Drama.

Brendan's response:

1 I am still very early career. I am in my final semester of graduate school and Humana is my first professional production, so the changes in my career really have yet to be determined. That said, I suppose I would count three real "breakthrough" moments in terms of the opportunities I've had so far. The first is being accepted to the playwriting program at Yale. The second is being commissioned to write the libretto for *Hagoromo*, a Japanese Noh-inspired chamber opera that premiered at BAM's Next Wave Festival this past fall—a job I got through a connection I made in a philosophy of aesthetics class I took audited at Yale Divinity School. The third is Humana, an opportunity that also feels like a homecoming because I was a literary department intern at the Actors Theatre of Louisville. All three opportunities have been important because they challenged me artistically, gave me the physical resources to see my work in three dimensions, and provided enough financial support to devote real time to my work.

2 Remains to be seen! I am currently at a residency working on a series of improvised radio plays with my longtime collaborator Natasha Haverty and working on some new play commissions.

John Pielmeier

John Pielmeier began his career with the play and movie *Agnes of God*, and most recently adapted *The Exorcist* for the stage. He has had four plays on Broadway, over 25 movies and miniseries on TV, and received the Humanitas, Edgar, Camie, and Christopher Awards, as well as five Writers Guild Award nominations. His first novel, *Hook's Tale,* has recently been published by Scribner. Please visit his website: johnpielmeier.com.

John's response:

1 My first professional break occurred when *Agnes of God* was accepted for development at the Eugene O'Neill Playwrights' Conference, but the circumstances leading up to that acceptance grew directly out of my earlier career as an actor. In April of 1977 I moved to New York from Minneapolis where I had been acting at the Guthrie. I got a call in May or June to audition for the O'Neill, initiated by a director whom I had met in Minnesota. I got the job, and at the O'Neill I a) befriended Arthur Ballet, a Minneapolis-based critic who had seen my acting work at the Guthrie and b) became entranced with the process at the O'Neill and decided that I wanted to return as a writer. I wrote a play that made the finals for the 1978 Conference, but not the final cut—Arthur was on the selection committee. That summer, instead of returning to the O'Neill, I wrote *Agnes*. It was accepted by the O'Neill the following year. Again, Arthur was on the selection committee, and I was known by the folks running the Conference. So my acceptance as a playwright had a lot to do with the physical places my acting had taken me, as well as with the people my acting had introduced me to. The same was later true of Actors Theatre of Louisville, where I had acted extensively and which gave the play its first professional production. In other words, it's so much about being in the right place and knowing the right people.

2 This second question is a tough one to answer. I can probably name two circumstances when I made a *bad* decision—both in choosing a director for one of my Broadway-bound plays. (The first choice I was pressured into by the producer, and it was a disastrous decision for us all. In the second instance I asked a friend to direct, and unhappiness ensued.) Recently I procrastinated about ridding myself of a useless agent, and suffered for it—another bad choice. Emotions run high when you're dealing with your babies, and it's difficult to make a wise and objective decision more often than not—at least for *me* it is. Good decisions? Hopefully, some decisions I've made recently were good ones, but time will tell. I've made some good casting decisions: the trio who did *Agnes* on Broadway, Judith Ivey in the Broadway production of my play *Voices in the Dark*, Harry Groener in a couple of other plays—and many other actors too numerous to mention, all of whom were co-chosen by the directors and producers. In general I guess that these decisions—both good and bad—are all small decisions at the time, but can often have a major impact on productions and career. Have I learned from them? Please God.

Jen Silverman

Jen Silverman is a New York-based playwright and writer. Her theatre work includes *The Moors* (Yale Repertory Theatre, Off-Broadway with The Playwrights Realm, Susan Smith Blackburn finalist); *The Roommate* (ATL, South Coast Repertory, upcoming at Williamstown Theatre Festival and Steppenwolf); and *Collective Rage: A Play in 5 Boops* (Woolly Mammoth, The Theater @ Boston Court), among others. Jen is a member of New Dramatists, a core writer at the Playwrights' Center in Minneapolis, a two-time MacDowell fellow, and the 2016–17 Playwrights of New York (PoNY) Fellow at the Lark.

Jen's response:

1 Going to grad school was the turning point for me. I was living in Japan, and the only thing that got me back to the US was getting into the Iowa Playwrights Workshop. I'd figured that if I was going to work a non-theatre job and write on the side, I might as well just stay in Japan, but the Workshop was a chance to really take the plunge and commit. So I moved to Iowa.

I know an MFA program isn't for everybody, but it changed my life. It was three years of unwavering, unflinching focus on craft, technique, story, aesthetic. Three years of being around truly exciting artists who were taking real risks. Three years of focusing on artistry over industry. The thing about Iowa, both pro and con, is that it's really far from New York. You don't know what's "in fashion" and you don't have agents coming to your readings, so you just buckle down and do the work of figuring out what you have to offer as a writer. Iowa has a number of student production opportunities so you aren't just writing into a vacuum—you're testing the work in 3D, on its feet, and both failures and successes are productive, they're giving you information about your voice and your craft and your collaborations.

By the time I left, I felt like I could say I was a playwright. A super-emerging, semi-fetal, lowest-rung-on-the-ladder playwright, sure. But I knew much more about myself as a writer, and I'd written fifteen full-length plays. (Of those fifteen, I've thrown out thirteen, so take this *only* as an example of how grad school gives space to rigorously practice.) The caveat I'll give though: never go to a grad program that leaves you in debt. It isn't worth it. The good ones have teaching fellowships, or are free.

2 I think it really comes down to having more than one thing to say—more than one thing that you *must* say, regardless of who is or isn't encouraging you. Just doing the work. It takes a long time to get any attention, and the frustration and despair can be crushing. So just write the next play. Don't wait for people to produce the first, second, third, etc. Don't wait to get into the fancy writers' group. Don't wait for permission to work. Just work.

Also, I learned not to be precious about the plays that don't quite work. Sometimes the value is in the practice and the experiment and getting to sharpen your tools, not the play itself. If you aren't being precious, you'll know when the play has value and deserves your attention, rewriting, rigor, development. And rewriting is vital—probably the best thing I learned at grad school was how and when to do it. No play spills out fully-formed and perfect; a good play demands the unglamorous grind of craft and dramaturgy, and multiple drafts.

Right after I moved to New York I spent a lot of time living in a tiny apartment in Queens, getting rejected from things and then writing the next play. Sometimes it felt like an exercise in futility, but I knew that if I stopped writing and started waiting for other people to say "yes" to me, I'd totally lose it. The funny thing is, the plays that I was banking on being produced (at that time) still haven't seen the light of day. And as for my play that was produced in Humana in 2015, I wrote *The Roommate* in May, Actor's Theatre of Louisville read the first draft and committed to the play in October, and it was produced in March, less than a year later. Which goes to show— the world is tricky, you can't second-guess politics and economics, all you can do is go deeper and write the next play.

Y York

Y York is the recipient of the Smith Prize for . . . *and LA Is Burning*; Houston's Buzzy Award for Best New Play for *Woof*; the Berrilla Kerr Award for *The Secret Wife*; the Hawai`i Award for Literature for *Nothing Is the Same*. Her plays have been supported by the National Endowment for the Arts, the Rockefeller Foundation, AT&T OnStage, United States Artists, and many local arts organizations through the years. For three decades she's been writing plays, most of which have been produced and more than twenty of which are published. Y still lives with Mark Lutwak, to whom all things are still dedicated.

Y's response:

One has to wonder what Jon means by "survive." Could he mean money: enough to pay the rent and the ever-expanding et cetera? Well, it's Jon, so one has to assume his meaning is not so prosaic. Perhaps by survive, he means persist, or persevere: How does the playwright make herself write the next play after the last one was: ignored, excoriated, botched, or worse—done so magnificently she knows she'll never write one that good again? The trick is that she's not watching, not waiting, not reading the press, but doing—ever in the process of making a new play, meeting a new theatre, enjoying some unknown other's work. "Forward ever, backward never" (quote of Maurice Bishop).

1 The third time was the charm for getting into New Dramatists. The first rejection was in-person and so mean I thought to write off ND and playwriting. (That rejecter wasn't with ND very long.) The second rejection was a form letter, anonymous, and, oddly, more painful. I kept writing plays and having off-Broadway readings of them, and applied again, got in, career got into gear, not fourth gear, but definitely not reverse (see Maurice Bishop quote above).

2 To leave New York. It was the best decision and the worst decision. New York is a blast, excitement abounds, distractions are legion, fun is everywhere, and on every playwright's radar is "career." New York playwrights talk a lot to one another, but the conversation is about opportunities and contacts, and, of course, good gossip. Had I stayed I might never have noticed that my plays needed work as did my artistry. Not-New-York doesn't have the fun (see above); it also doesn't have the distractions. No one was asking to read it, so I wasn't rushing the new play. I learned to take my time, how to take my play apart; I assembled my criteria for excellence and started to share my knowledge. The most important gift of Not-New-York: I got introduced to some new kinds of audiences who changed my writing and who also changed me. As to evaluating the decision, see the Maurice Bishop quote above.

11 Final Thoughts

By now I hope I've given you an informed indication about a life as a playwright. I'd like to finish up with a final list of lessons and tips, based mostly on my own experiences. Here goes, with a few points I may or may not have mentioned before:

- **Learn about other writers, but don't imitate them. Developing your own voice is essential to achieving recognition.**

- **You don't learn as much from the finished production as you do from the rehearsal process.**

- **You can't ever be completely sure of what's on the page. Dramatic writing needs to be heard out loud, and preferably workshopped with actors in performance, for truly successful results.**

- **Learning how to work together with actors and directors is a skill that is equally important to writing a good script. Maybe more so!**

- **Isolation as a writer is pointless and damaging. The social and community aspects of theatre—ones that gather a specific group of people together for a common purpose—are essential to encourage and accommodate.**

- **Learning how to listen and incorporate constructive feedback is essential to good collaboration. But so is the ability to stand up for what you know to be true about your own writing. It's quite possible to do both, despite the apparent conflict.**

And I'll separate the last one, because it is the most important:

- **Playwriting is a difficult profession (notice I'm still reluctant to use the word "career"). And the rewards tend to be more emotionally satisfying than financial. But only you can tell if you're born to be a playwright. You'll know the first time you get thrown from the horse. Will you brush yourself off, climb back on and try again? Or will you wish the horse well and start thumbing your way back to a life that takes fewer risks?**

Believe me, I'm no risk taker myself, and there were many occasions when I wondered why I was even trying to *have* a life in the theatre. I guess the simple answer is that I could never imagine doing anything else.

Can you?

Works Cited

Albee, Edward (1966), *Zoo Story*, Copenhagen: Gyldendal.

An Officer and a Gentleman. Dir. Taylor Hackford. Paramount Pictures, 1982.

Anouilh, Jean, and Lucienne Hill (1960), *Becket, Or, The Honour of God: A Play in Four Acts*, New York: S. French.

Ball, David, and Michael Langham (1988), *Backwards and Forwards: A Technical Manual for Reading Plays*, Carbondale: Southern Illinois UP.

Beckett, Samuel (1954), *Waiting for Godot: Tragicomedy in 2 Acts*, New York: Grove.

Beckett, Samuel (1960), *Krapp's Last Tape: And Other Dramatic Pieces*, New York: Grove.

Beckett, Samuel (1983), *Worstward Ho*, New York: Grove.

Berlioz, Hector, Léon De Wailly, and Auguste Barbier (1963), *Benvenuto Cellini; Opera in 3 Acts*, London: Oxford UP.

Bernstein, Leonard, Hugh Wheeler, Richard Wilbur, John Latouche, Stephen Sondheim, and Voltaire (1973), *Candide*, New York: Souvenir Book.

Cellini, Benvenuto, and John Addington Symonds (1927), *The Autobiography of Benvenuto Cellini*, New York: Modern Library.

Coburn, D. L. (1978), *The Gin Game*, New York: Drama Book Specialists.

Connelly, Marc (1930), *The Green Pastures, a Fable*, New York: Farrar & Rinehart.

D'Andrea, Paul, and Jon Klein (2005), *The Einstein Project*, New York, Dramatists Play Service.

Devil's Advocate, The. Dir. Taylor Hackford, 1997.

Doctorow, E. L. (1975), *Ragtime*, New York: Random House.

Edson, Margaret (1999), *Wit: A Play*, New York: Faber and Faber.

Fitzgerald, F. Scott (1920), *This Side of Paradise*, New York: Scribner.

Fitzgerald, F. Scott (1925), *The Great Gatsby*, New York: Scribner.

Galand, Joel, Ira Gershwin, and Edwin Justus Mayer (2002), *The Firebrand of Florence: Broadway Operetta in Two Acts*, New York: Kurt Weill Foundation for Music.

Get Shorty. Dir. Barry Sonnenfeld, 1995.

Goldman, James (1966), *The Lion in Winter*, New York: Random House.

Goldman, William (1983), *Adventures in the Screen Trade: A Personal View of Hollywood and Screenwriting*, New York: Warner.

Hart, Moss (1959), *Act One: An Autobiography*, New York: Random House.

Hatcher, Jeffrey (2000), *The Art & Craft of Playwriting*, Cincinnati, OH: Story.

Healey, Patrick (2010), "Playwrights' Nurturing Is the Focus of a Study," *New York Times,* January 13: n. pag.

Henley, Beth (1982), *Crimes of the Heart: A Play*, New York: Viking.

Hirson, Roger O., and Stephen Schwartz (1977), *Pippin: A Musical Comedy*, New York: Avon.

Hombre. Dir. Martin Ritt, 1967.

Joseph, Rajiv (2013), *Bengal Tiger at the Baghdad Zoo*, New York: Dramatists Play Service.

Kierkegaard, Søren, David F. Swenson, and Walter Lowrie (1941), *Kierkegaard's Concluding Unscientific Postscript*, Princeton: Princeton UP, for American-Scandinavian Foundation.

Kirkwood, James, with Michael Bennett, Nicholas Dante, and Edward Kleban (1975), *A Chorus Line*, New York: Applause Theatre and Cinema Books.

Klein, Jon (1987), *T Bone N Weasel*, New York: Dramatists Play Service.

Klein, Jon (1991), *Southern Cross*, New York: Dramatists Play Service.

Klein, Jon (1999), *Dimly Perceived Threats to the System*, New York: Dramatists Play Service.

Klein, Jon (n.d.), *Losing It: A Comedy*, n.p.: n.p.

Klein, Jon (n.d.), *Octopus*, n.p.: n.p.

Klein, Jon, and Stendhal (1993), *The Red and the Black: A Stage Adaptation of the Stendhal Novel*, Seattle: Rain City Projects.

Kopit, Arthur (1969), *Indians; a Play*, New York: Hill & Wang.

Larson, Jonathan (2008), *Rent*, New York: Applause Theatre & Cinema Books; Applause Books edition.

Leigh, Mitch, Joe Darion, and Dale Wasserman (1966), *Man of La Mancha; a Musical Play*, New York: Random House.

London, Todd, Ben Pesner, and Zannie Giraud Voss (2009), *Outrageous Fortune: The Life and Times of the New American Play*, New York: Theatre Development Fund.

Murray, John, and Allen Boretz (1937), *Room Service*, New York: Random House.

Nelson, Victoria (1993), *On Writer's Block: A New Approach to Creativity*, New York: Houghton Mifflin.

Norman, Marsha (1979), *Getting Out*, Garden City, NY: Nelson Doubleday.

Norman, Marsha (1983), *'Night, Mother: A Play*, New York: Hill and Wang.

Nottage, Lynn (2009), *Ruined*, New York: Theatre Communications Group.

O'Neill, Eugene (1952), *A Moon for the Misbegotten, a Play in Four Acts*, New York: Random House.

Out of Sight. Dir. Steven Soderbergh, 1998.

Rabe, David (1975), *In the Boom Boom Room*, New York: Knopf.

Rado, James, with Jerome Ragni and Gail McDermott (1969), *Hair*. United Artists Music Co. Inc.

Ray. Dir. Taylor Hackford. Universal Pictures, 2005.

Reza, Yasmina, and Christopher Hampton (1996), *Art*, London: Faber and Faber.

Reza, Yasmina, and Christopher Hampton (2008), *The God of Carnage*, London: Faber and Faber.

Samuels, Steven (1994), "Interview with Edward Albee," *American Theatre*, September 1: n. pag. Web.

Schwartz, Stephen, and Roger O. Hirson (1975), *Pippin: A Musical Comedy*, New York: Drama Book Specialists.

Shaffer, Peter (1975), *Equus: A Play*, New York: Avon.

Shakespeare, William, and Davis P. Harding (1954), *Measure for Measure*, New Haven: Yale University Press.

Shanley, John Patrick, and Benvenuto Cellini (2002), *Cellini*, New York: Dramatists Play Service.

Shepard, Sam (1982), *True West*, Garden City, NY: Nelson Doubleday.

Stendhal, C. K. Scott-Moncrieff, and Rafaello Busoni (1947), *The Red and the Black*, New York: Heritage.

Stoppard, Tom (1975), *Travesties*, New York: Grove Press.

Stump, Rebecca, ed. (2016), *Dramatists Guild Resource Directory*, New York: Lulu Press, Inc.

T Bone N Weasel. Dir. Lewis Teague. Turner Network Television, 1992.

The Producers. Dir. Mel Brooks. 1968.

The Wedding Singer. Dir. Frank Coraci. 1998.

Tootsie. Dir. Sydney Pollack. 1982.

Toy Story. Dir. John Lasseter. Disney/Pixar, 2010.

Wasserman, Dale, and Ken Kesey (1974), *One Flew over the Cuckoo's Nest: A Play in Two Acts*, New York: S. French.

Webber, Andrew Lloyd, John Napier, and T. S. Eliot (1983), *Cats: The Book of the Musical: Based on Old Possum's Book of Practical Cats by T.S. Eliot*, San Diego: Harcourt Brace Jovanovich.

Weiss, Peter, Geoffrey Skelton, Adrian Mitchell, Peter Brook, and Richard Peaslee (1965), *The Persecution and Assassination of Jean-Paul Marat as Performed by the Inmates of the Asylum of Charenton under the Direction of the Marquis De Sade*, New York: Atheneum.

Weller, Michael (1972), *Moonchildren*, New York: Delacorte.

Williams, Tennessee (1947), *A Streetcar Named Desire: A Play*, New York: New Directions.

Williams, Tennessee (2006), *Memoirs*, New York: New Directions.

Wright, Doug, Amanda Green, and Trey Anastasio (n.d.), *Hands on a Hardbody*, n.p.: n.p.

About the Author

Jon Klein is the author of over thirty produced plays, performed at Off-Broadway and at many prestigious regional theatres, including the Humana Festival, Arena Stage in DC, and the Alliance Theater in Atlanta. His plays have been developed and workshopped at Sundance, PlayLabs, New York Stage & Film, and the Kennedy Center. Jon has taught playwriting and screenwriting at UCLA, the University of Texas, the University of Washington, Ohio University, and Hollins University. He is currently the head of the MFA Playwriting Program at Catholic University of America in Washington, DC.

Website: www.jon-klein.com

Published Plays by Jon Klein

Dramatists Play Service

Betty the Yeti
Dimly Perceived Threats to the System
Southern Cross
T Bone n Weasel
The Einstein Project (co-authored with Paul D'Andrea)

Broadway Play Publishing

Suggestibility
Wishing Well
Young Robin Hood

Plays for Young Audiences

Bunnicula

Samuel French

Four Our Fathers

Index